Growing Up BLACK in WHITE

KEVIN D. HOFMANN

ISBN: 0-578-05150-8
ISBN-13: 978-0-578-05150-5

God is the reason this book was made possible. I would like to dedicate this book to God, the one who chose me to live out such an interesting life. Looking at my life it is easy to see God's watermark.

I would also like to dedicate this book to my parents. The sacrifices you made for me are humbling.

Lastly, I would like to dedicate this book to my wife and two sons. Thanks for giving up quality time so I could retrace my life and do the work I was created to do.

TABLE OF CONTENTS

1

WELCOME

The flames shoot skyward and claw at the moon. The orange and yellow tongues of fire dance above the shades of blue. I am still sound asleep in my crib enjoying the last moments of blessed peace. At 11 months old I am cocooned in the land of dreams and unwilling to leave.

It's the summer of 1968 and these flames are coming from the front yard of our Monroe Street home in Dearborn, Michigan, a small suburb of Detroit. The sound of voices on the front lawn in the early summer morning hours bring Mom and Dad out of their restful sleep. Mom springs out of bed when she sees the reflections of the flames on the ceiling and walls of her second story bedroom. At the window she only sees a blurry glow of fire below. She doesn't take the time to get her glasses so her vision is limited to shadows and flickering lights. Her mind recognizes it is fire, but her near-sighted eyes can't focus as to what is on fire.

My three siblings join me in undisturbed sleep; each in our own beds across the hall. The mother instincts tears at her chest. She is conflicted between running to the phone to call for help and running to her four children to protect them. The phone is downstairs and her children are upstairs. Instead, Mom dispatches Dad to check on us while she races to the phone downstairs.

As Mom exits her room she grabs her glasses purposely dodging the windows in case the voices are looking for a human target. As she goes down the stairs and turns to the right, she hurries into the den and picks up the heavy Bell telephone and dials "0."

The answer to the question that is racing around in her head still has not come. What is on fire? Trying to put together thoughts is nearly impossible. Panic and fear whirl inside her head. Mom wants to cry and scream for help but no one but the perpetrators will hear her.

The trip down the stairs brings her closer to the fire and it seems to be right outside the window and moving quickly towards the house. The bright shadows and confusion tell a convincing story. As Mom is waiting for the help on the other end of the phone to pick up, she digests the information and is certain the fire is consuming the wooden plantation style porch. Soon the fire will find its way in to the house and the owners of the voices may not be too far behind.

The operator picks up the phone and Mom pleads for help desperately wishing they could send the help through the phone lines. Instead, the emotionless operator assures her help is on the way. As she returns the phone to the cradle, she prays the operator will respect the panic in her voice and send help right away.

Climbing back up the stairs to Dad and the kids, Mom is relieved to move away from the fire and invisible voices. Dad meets Mom at the top of the steps. Relief washes over Mom when she hears all four kids are asleep and have no knowledge of the front yard fireworks. The pace of the morning chaos slows down considerably with Dad's report.

Mom and Dad return to their room to get a better view of the fire below. Their aerial view brings a harsh clarity to the situation. The fire comes from a six foot high cross in the middle of their spacious front lawn. The flames roil and the crackle of burning wood is all that can be heard. The invisible voices have disappeared leaving their glowing calling card

The apartment building next door begins to awaken. The dark windows of the apartments begin to flash one by one against the night backdrop. As each light pops on, the feeling of isolation is driven further away.

Another flash appears as the exterior door to the apartment building is pushed open. The bright light across the dark yard outlines the silhouette of a young man. He marches quickly and with purpose to the burning cross that is fading away. The march pours into a jog and then a run as he approaches the cross. As he zeros in on his target he leaps feet first into the cross. His perfectly targeted kick to the base of the cross causes it to crash to the ground. The impact forces glowing wood and sparks to jump in to the air. The young man turns sharply and walks back into the light from the open door. He slams the door behind him and the street is now early-morning quiet again.

After 45 minutes the Dearborn police arrive. They ask the necessary questions to complete their report and then they leave. Mom and Dad are not comforted by their presence nor are they convinced any investigation will occur beyond the paper report.

As the sun rises on the charred and broken cross, my parents replay the last eight months of candid feedback from neighbors and disapproving glances. It doesn't take them long to wonder who initiated the visit, even if the neighbors weren't actually the ones to strike the match. What Mom and Dad did has shaken up their small community and the community was now shaking them back.

In November of 1967, my parents brought me home for the first time. I travel from a foster home in the neighboring city of Detroit to the parsonage occupied by Mom, Dad, and their three children. Dad is a white associate pastor at the nearby, all-white, Lutheran church. Mom is a busy homemaker who attends to three children five years old and younger. Now added to the mix is me a three-month old bi-racial child. My presence in that house starts a controversy no one would have predicted.

Being a pastor and the wife of a pastor, my adoptive parents, strive to live what their Christian faith taught them. When someone is in need you help him. When someone needs a helping hand you offer yours. Unfortunately, Dearborn is not a city of pastors and we will soon learn not all pastors and/or Christians are eager to extend their hands.

I laugh today when I see large wooden animals in a neighbor's yard that has been erected to celebrate an important event. They usually have a catchy sign attached to it that says something like, "Lordy, Lordy, Cathy's 40," or "Oh joy, it's a boy." This is a way for people to acknowledge and publicly celebrate something. Then I think back to the wooden welcome I got in Dearborn.

It is usually easy to select a gift when someone has a baby. You bring them diapers, sippy cup or maybe a play pen. When someone gets married it's even easier. They have a list to pick from at a local store. The dilemma comes when a white family, in one of the whitest cities in America during the Civil Rights Movement, brings home a biracial child. What do you do to make an 11-month-old biracial boy feel welcome?

A flaming cross seems like the perfect way to say "WELCOME TO DEARBORN."

To understand why and how an irrational fear sounds so rational to so many, you have to realize what is going on in 1968 in Southeast Michigan. You have to go back twelve months to the summer of 1967.

In the summer of 1967, Detroit is diagnosed with an inoperable cancer three weeks before I take my first breath. In the early morning hours of July 23, 1967 the city rises to a disease that could no longer contain itself. What begins as a celebration rages into a full-blown insurrection that is recorded on national TV.

At the corner of Twelfth Street and Clairmont on Detroit's northwest side (a predominately black neighborhood) several gather on this Saturday night/early Sunday morning to celebrate two Vietnam vets returning home from the war. The welcome home party takes place in an illegal after-hours club.

As the alcohol is poured and glasses are raised to toast the heroes, Motown music shares the air with cigarette smoke and oxygen. Martha Reeves and the Vandellas are asking when Jimmy Mack is coming back. Their question floats on the dense air. Marvin Gay and Tammi Terrell are singing back and forth about a love that can't be contained by a mountain, no matter how high; and the Four Tops harmonize about sweet Bernadette.

At about 3:30 a.m. on Sunday morning, the Detroit Police Department, which is mostly white, joins the party. Their plan is to raid the after hours club and arrest the patrons inside. The first police on the scene find more partygoers then they expect so they call for additional support and wait. While they wait for back up, a crowd begins to gather from the neighborhood. The tension begins to swell in this black community as years and years of mistreatment by whites, lack of opportunity and disrespect, have pushed the community closer and closer to its boiling point. On this early morning the blacks in Detroit would voice in unison they have had enough.

On the corner of Twelfth and Clairmont there is assembled a crowd that is too restless, too sick, and too tired to sleep. They chose to turn their attention and frustration to local businesses and property instead. The sweet sounds of Motown are replaced with angry chants and the ping of breaking glass. Fires crackle and the suffocating smell of burning buildings and furniture replace the recent smell of alcohol. Within hours, the destruction consumes the neighborhood and spills over into the surrounding neighborhoods as the angry crowds grow.

People watch helplessly as the fires greedily eat up property in neighborhoods deemed too dangerous for the fire department to enter.

Soon the National Guard arrives to help control the unrest. The National Guard marches down the streets of Detroit with weapons at their side. The troops are escorted by armed tanks. They are dressed for war in the middle of a city and Detroit quickly transforms into a war zone. The presence of the National Guard only adds fuel to an already uncontrollable fire.

The riots rage for five days. When the streets calm 43 people are dead, 8200 are arrested, 823 are injured and 2500 businesses or homes are burned to the ground*. Detroit lay quiet and smoldering. Cut open from chin to navel and there exposed on national TV is a massive tumor that had been growing and was untreated for decades in Detroit.

Two and a half weeks after the raid at Twelfth Street, in Martin Place West Hospital, I am born. I emerge from my white mother, put there by my black father in a time where different pigments can't get along. Fortunately for me, hormones trump pigment.

Thirty-five years after this series of events unfolded, I sat down with Mom and Dad and they shared with me their early memories of my life with them. For the first time I hear the fiery cross story and I am humbled.

Being adopted brings with it the special feeling of being specifically chosen by your adoptive family. My special feeling walked hand in hand with the guilt that I felt for being the cause of such turmoil.

Being a parent by definition means sacrifice but what my parents endured was Herculean. I often reflect back at this scene and that time and I marvel at the couple who chose to bring color to a city that did not want to be colorized. I marvel at their courage to do what was right when all around them told them it was wrong.

My birth occurred in the middle of this racial hurricane. In my veins flows black and white created in a time when the lines were clearly drawn. These lines were so boldly outlined and no one was to cross them, yet my birth parents ignored those lines and created me. Again, I am humbled but at the same time I feel so very special.

It is my belief that each adoptee is divinely matched and placed with their adoptive family. As my parents continued to tell me the story of how I arrived in their care, this belief is confirmed. As they welcomed me in to their home, I beat the odds no Las Vegas bookie would ever bet on.

2

GOD ODDS

The odds of eating an oyster and finding a pearl: **1 in 12,000.**

The odds of being struck by lighting: 1 **in 200,000.**

The odds of getting pregnant with quadruplets: **1 in 705,000.**

What are the odds of a biracial baby up for adoption in Detroit getting placed in a permanent home in 1967?

In early 1967, a Lutheran minister, Pastor Hofmann, and his wife set out to complete their family. They have been blessed with three healthy children to this point but the physical toll on the wife after the third pregnancy meant the fourth child would have to come by way of adoption.

The pastor and his wife contacted a private adoption agency to complete their family plan. In early 1967 the couple begins the climb up and over the mountain of paperwork, the thorough background checks and the necessary home visits. One by one the required items are scratched off the list and the couple is approved for adoption.

Then they wait.

The 1967 tulips bloom and die. The late spring winds blow through the large trees on Monroe Street. The summer grass comes in creating a natural carpet for children to play. Teenage boys walk behind push mowers. Then baseball games start and end as August passes. Rakes replace the mowers and the same able-bodied homeowners exchange aching lawn mowing muscles for aching raking muscles.

And still the couple waits for their baby.

The sun comes out less and less. A riot begins and ends six miles away and a city is changed forever. It is close enough to be scary, but in 1967, six miles to Detroit is a lifetime away.

The phone in the Hofmann household sits quiet.

In the summer of 1967, I was born. My birth mother has some connection to the Lutheran faith; therefore I am placed with a private agency instead of the state. 21 years after this placement I find out my birth mother has no connection with the Lutheran faith. My placement with a private agency versus the state means the odds of my placement into a permanent home got substantially better.

I am placed in a foster home on the West side of Detroit in the care of my foster mother Mrs. Curry, a gentle and caring black woman in her sixties. She is married and she and Mr. Curry name me David and give me my first home

As I settle in to my new home, Mrs. Hofmann, the wife of Pastor Hofmann, dials the number to the adoption agency located in downtown Detroit. Mrs. Hofmann has grown tired of all the waiting with no answers. She is put in touch with the director who explains that the right child has not come along yet. The director explains that since the couple has qualified for a "hard to place" child the search isn't as easy. This is the first time Mrs. Hofmann has heard the phrase "hard to place child" so the young mother asks what that means exactly. It is explained since the couple already has their own children they will have to accept a child that is harder to place.

The director explains she does have a child that qualifies, if they are interested. The child is a baby girl who was born with a heart defect; a hole in the heart. The director goes on to explain this special needs child will need extensive medical attention for many years and there is no guarantee the child will survive.

The couple thinks it over for a few days. They consider the attention, the emotional expense and the financial expense. The care for this child will be very taxing to all areas. They already have three children and on a pastor's salary there is not a lot of extra room. All the medical expenses for their children to date are taken care of by a charitable pediatrician who understands the wallet size of a preacher. This little girl is simply a mountain the Hofmanns can't climb.

They call the director to explain the little girl is not a challenge they are able to take on. The director understands and inquires if they would be interested in a different kind of "hard to place" child. She explains that biracial children also qualify as "hard to place."

The races in the late sixties in Detroit are so polarized that neither race wants a child with part of the other's race. The whites want a white child and the blacks want a black child; therefore a biracial child in Detroit, Michigan in 1967 qualifies as "hard to place."

To even pose this question is a risk, but the director has to lob it out there to see if they will swing at it. For her, it is a safe risk. This is a Christian family after all, how can they object?

Her gamble pays off. The couple graciously agrees to put biracial on their list. The director goes back to work to find the right child and the waiting begins again.

The postman brings hope sealed in an invitation delivered one day in November. The invitation comes from the adoption agency. They are having a tea at their main office on West Grand Boulevard in Detroit. The tea is designed to bring potential parents, potential foster parents, current foster parents, and children up for adoption together. It is created to spark interest in becoming foster parents; to hopefully match up parents with adoptees and show what services the agency has to offer. The Hofmanns put the date on their calendar and plan to attend.

The coveted date arrives and they make their way to the main office of the adoption agency. Inside there is a large room with rows and rows of folding chairs that take over the middle of the room. People speak politely in the way most people do when they are nervous and unsure what else to do. It is easy to tell the potential parents from the foster parents. There is energy in the eyes of the potential parents. There is a special way their smiles curl. The Hofmanns have that look.

As the small groups break up and everyone takes their seat, they begin to circulate the foster children around the room. The hopeful parents handle, admire and burp children like they are containers at a Tupperware party.

That day my foster mother, Mrs. Curry exits her home shortly after she dresses me for the cool Detroit November air. I arrive in the room and Mrs. Curry knows the drill. She has been a foster mother for many years and I am sure she has been to plenty of teas. She surrenders me shortly after entering the room and sends me on my journey. I too am passed from one set of waiting arms to another. As I land in the arms of Mrs. Hofmann, the director of the agency strolls by and remarks, "This would be the perfect baby for you if he were only a girl." Distracted by the excitement of our first meeting, the Hofmanns don't process what the director has said. They hold me for a few moments and then politely send me on my way down the row.

I continue on my publicity junket as Mr. and Mrs. Hofmann process the comment the director made. The confused hopeful parents turn to each other and asked the same question. "Who told her we were only interested in a girl?"

As the tea concludes the Hofmanns approach the director and ask where she got the idea that they only wanted a girl. She innocently and independently thought since they already had two boys and one girl, they needed another girl to make the family symmetrical.

Humbly the Hofmanns explain they would be interested in adding another boy to their family. In particular, they are interested in the child whom the director thought would be perfect for them, even if he was a boy. The Hofmann's formally inquire about making me a part of their family. The director schedules an appointment with the Hofmanns to sit down and discuss the possibilities of adopting me.

The date of the scheduled appointment comes and the Hofmanns arrive to discuss the next step in the process. They sit at her desk and are informed that I am available for adoption. The director only has to verify if I have had a recent trip to the pediatrician. It is standard procedure to confirm the health of the child before the adoption can be finalized. The director calls my caseworker as the Hofmanns sit waiting for the news. Although they can only hear one end of the conversation, it is evident by the tone of the "oh, yes I see" that the response to her question isn't positive. When she hangs up the phone, she confirms I have not recently been seen by a pediatrician. In fact, my last medical evaluation was three months ago during my short stay at Martin Place West Hospital.

The Hofmann's sit at the desk disappointed not knowing how long this will delay things. At the rate that things had moved to that point, it could mean months and months of red tape. It could mean months of worrying about this child's health and if he would also need extensive care. This answer could have meant so many possibilities; too many possibilities.

"Why don't you go pick him up from his foster home and have him looked at by your pediatrician? If he checks out you can keep him." The director says.

"What if there is something wrong with him?" asks Mrs. Hofmann.

"Just bring him back." This is the reply that comes back without a pause.

"Just take him home and try him out. If he doesn't work out just bring him back," the director encourages. She does not see the absurdity in her comments. She is just anxious to close a deal that isn't expected to get closed.

The offer that is presented doesn't sit level. It seems to lean to one side but it is not clear to what side it leans. The generosity in the offer makes it appear to be genuine. The idea that some rule or procedure is being ignored causes the offer to tilt more towards the left. The nagging feeling that this deal shouldn't be made, in this way, causes the Hofmanns to pause.

While they debate the unusual offer, the director pushed the conversation forward. She sees the impossible is actually possible and she does not want to waste a second for "no" to creep in. She pushes the paperwork forward as she places a call to Mrs. Curry. The phone call is quick and concise, just enough time to get the needed information.   She returns the phone back to its cradle and advises Mrs. Curry will have me ready momentarily. The Hofmanns are shuffled out of her office, given directions to Mrs. Curry's residence, and congratulated all in a matter of seconds.

The Hofmanns are half way to Mrs. Curry's before they realize what took place. The signing of papers occurred somewhere in this organized confusion. As they signed the last "n" in Hofmann they are transformed from Mr. & Mrs. Hofmann to my Mom and Dad.

The offer is never contemplated or discussed. The Hofmanns decide separately and silently once they pick me up I will be permanently placed; in their family.

They pull up to Mrs. Curry's home on Birwood Street. As promised, Mrs. Curry has me packed and ready to go. My foster mother is soft spoken, respectful and kind as she gently hands me over. The bewildered new parents reach for me and Mrs. Curry's reassuring smile passes over to them hope; the kind of hope that assures them everything will be ok.

The odds of a biracial child up for adoption being placed in a permanent home in Detroit in 1967: insurmountable. The odds of this union coming together were God odds; odds only God could overcome. On that November afternoon, God places me in the arms of the family that he chooses just for me. Getting others to agree on God's placement would also be insurmountable.

3

HEART BROKEN

Eight years before I am placed in my Mom and Dad's arms, Grandpa grabs the phone as it rings in their Grosse Pointe Michigan home. On the other end of the phone is the nightshift supervisor at the Budd Company plant in Detroit. The supervisor is asking Grandpa to come in and help with a situation they are having at the plant.

Grandpa has gained a reputation of being able to handle '"them" and this time "they' are out of control. The "they" and "them" are the blacks who work on the line at Budd. Tonight the line is shut down due to a mechanical problem. Usually when the line is shut down "they" retreat to the men's bathroom and set up shop while the problem is repaired.

Tonight, constructed in the small washroom, is a miniature bar with alcohol and drugs. "They" take the doors off the stalls, lay them on the floor and use them to shoot dice.

The party reaches its pinnacle just as the horn sounds calling them back to the line. The machine is fixed. When management insists they get back to work, "they" refuse and it gets back to management someone may have a gun. Management panics and calls Grandpa to assist.

Grandpa hangs up the phone and heads out the door. He is on his way to see if he can work his magic and get "them" to behave. As he drives into the parking lot, one of the "goodies" (the blacks that behaved, but not enough to be considered outside of "they.") approaches Grandpa. "Don't go in der boss, they gonna kill ya." Grandpa ignores the warning and marches into the plant and straight into the homemade bar. He jumps up on the urinal and tells "them' to wrap it up, close the bar and get back to work and "they" do. Grandpa leaves as quickly as he came and returns home.

He would later tell Grandma he was shaking as he stood on the urinal and shouted. He admitted he came close to leaving a deposit in the urinal he was standing on. Fortunately, Grandpa got the line up and running proving he knew how to handle "them."

This is the story my Grandmother relays to me as I interview her for this book. These are her terms and her account. I am not sure how accurate it is, but it is entertaining. Hearing her tell the story with no apologies and unaware how offensive her version is, I am entertained. I am entertained by her view of blacks. It sounds like she is telling a story about some wild animals that had gotten loose and Grandpa, the animal trainer, was called in to round "em" up and he did it absent a chair or a whip.

Mom grew up in Philadelphia Pennsylvania, the daughter of Grandpa, the "animal trainer". In their house there were lines drawn around races and one race was seen as superior to another. This mentality was handed down to Mom but Mom chose not to imitate it.

This is seen very clearly in a gift that was given to Mom when she was a young girl. On one special occasion Mom was given a black doll named "Niggy." The origin of the doll or how the doll got its name Mom couldn't remember but Niggy was an accepted part of her early childhood.

In this same house Mom was not allowed to bring home a black friend from school because in their house blacks were not allowed unless you were stuffed and named Niggy or Juanita the "colored" cleaning lady who came once a week .

In this house, referring to blacks as "they," and "them" was ok.

In this house this was the accepted talk and attitudes that many had at that time. It was so a part of Grandma that she never let it go and never saw it as wrong. Even when sharing stories with her biracial grandson.

On November 14, 1967, I am carried across the threshold into my new house. I am three months old and already in my second home. There to greet me are my new brothers and sister, who had no idea I was coming home today. My big sister Lisa and big brothers, James and Matthew are there full of grins and smiles. I am placed on the dining room table in my bassinet like an early Thanksgiving turkey and all our eyes shine with excitement. We are instant siblings and they don't even know what to call me. Lisa suggests the name Kevin, after a young boy she was so fond of in elementary school. All agree and I am given the name Kevin. David, the name given to me by my foster mother, becomes my middle name.

During the excitement of the next few days, Mom's excitement splits time with fear. Her parents are on their way to Dearborn. Mom is concerned with how her old house will receive her new house.

In those quiet hours, Mom and I rock in the black wooden rocking chair that Grandpa made with his own hands. As Mom feeds me, I am sure she was reminded of Niggy, the doll she pretended to feed and rock to sleep many years before. It was a thought that came back to her often in those first few days.

Grandpa and Grandma's journey to this point was a busy one. Grandpa was transferred from the foundry with the Budd Company in Philadelphia to the Budd plant in Detroit. After nine years with Budd in Detroit, his fondness for alcohol brought the job to a quick end. From there, Grandpa found a job as a consultant for a foundry in India. He and Grandma moved to India for three years. After three years, his bottle cut that job short too. Their first stop back in the states is in Dearborn to see my Mom and Dad, and the newly expanded family.

The overseas communication is minimal so Grandma and Grandpa only know part of the adoption story. They know Mom and Dad are going to adopt the fourth child, but they don't know when and they are unaware of the "hard to place" twist. They find out just how special I am the second they peer in to my bassinet. The long distance makes it convenient; a good excuse not to have an uncomfortable conversation.

At our introduction, I am placed in Grandma's arms and she stares at me. Shock dissolves what little inhibitions Grandma has and she quickly asks, "Well, what is he? He looks Indian!"

My fair skin and racial makeup produce what Grandma thinks is a child that looks like he is from India. She passes me to Grandpa without saying much else and he quickly agrees, "Boy, he does look like an Indian baby." Sitting in Grandma's apartment, Grandma, and I reminisce about the 35 years of my life leading up to the day of this interview. Grandpa is no longer with us and in the same manner as she tells the plant story she tells all her stories. No apologies, no concessions. Grandma continues as she proudly tells me the story of my baptism.

It is a few weeks after our first meeting. Grandma and Grandpa are still visiting in Dearborn when Mom and Dad schedule my baptism.

The head pastor of the church does not share Mom and Dad's enthusiasm for diversity. Instead, he refuses to baptize me. He doesn't want to support my presence in the city or in his church in any way. The younger pastor, who was also an assistant with Dad, sees no problem with it and agrees to baptize me. The head pastor reluctantly agrees to allow me to be baptized.

The morning of my baptism Dad comes back to the house after the first service to say the head pastor has changed his mind. Now he will not allow the baptism at all, no matter who does it. Mom and Dad are surprised but not shocked. The pastor has made it very clear what he thinks of their choice in children.

Dad tells Mom to bring me to the later service ready to be baptized and Dad returns to church to try and convince his pastor to change his mind.

We arrive at the late service, and the baptism is now on again. Dad somehow convinces the head pastor to allow my baptism. I am baptized by the younger assistant pastor. Grandma sits in the pew intensely watching Mom as I am being baptized. She can see the redness that flows to Mom's cheeks; the same redness that attacks Mom's face when she eats spicy foods. She can see Mom's jaw contract as she grits her teeth hoping no one will stand up and oppose the baptism. Fortunately, there isn't the opportunity in a baptism for someone to "speak now or forever hold their peace."

As soon as I am baptized, the redness in Mom's cheeks and tight jaw wash away. Mom carries me back to the pew and places me in Grandma's arms. Throughout the whole service I don't make a sound; not even when they pour the water on my head. Grandma sits holding the Indian-looking baby beaming with pride.

The prideful moment doesn't last long. It is interrupted by the noticeable tension that fills the church. Since my introduction to the church there has been a growing debate between those who support my presence and those that don't. Up until my baptism those that opposed my inclusion in the church would gather in small circles and discuss why my presence should not be allowed. Those that supported my inclusion would do the same. The two opposing groups never came together, until today. The issue that they disagreed about was lying in Mom's arm in front of the church. Anyone scanning the faces in the crowd as I am baptized could easily tell who stood on what side of this debate. After Church, Grandma and Grandpa go straight back to our house. They don't stay to socialize over coffee and doughnuts because the tense environment makes Grandma nauseous.

Grandma and Grandpa stay for a few more weeks and then they leave for Chicago to go spend time with Grandma's sister. They would soon settle in Florida in a house Grandpa would build.

A year later, Grandma and Grandpa return for another visit. They are afraid for their daughter after they hear about the cross burning incident that took place a few months before.

They worry about the daughter who has four kids all under the age of six to take care of. Grandma is afraid the attacks will become more personal and someone in her daughter's family might get killed. In the past year, the assassinations of Dr. Martin Luther King and Bobby Kennedy take place, so the fear that someone could be killed is very real.

Grandma is simply a mother worrying about the safety of her daughter.

During their visit, Mom returns home from a trip to her hairdresser. She is visibly upset and her hair is unchanged. Grandma asks what's wrong, and Mom explains, through her tears, that her hairdresser refused to cut her hair. When Mom asked why, the hairdresser explained it was because she had us kids with her. Mom had been there several times with three out of the four of us and nothing was ever said. Mom had been there when other customers had their children with them and nothing was ever said. It was the first and last time I made the trip to that hairdresser.

Embarrassed and furious Mom left the hairdresser and came home. By now, Mom is used to this type of confrontation and on any other day it wouldn't have bothered her. On this day, she had enough, enough of the same old thing, enough of the ugliness. It was just enough to make her crack. But there is no better time to crack than when your mother is around. Your mother is there to help cushion your fall during times like these. When Mom finishes her story, she asks in between her sobs, "What am I going to do?"

Grandma's own fears and frustrations over this adoption make if difficult for Grandma to see her crying daughter in front of her. Grandma is trying to sort out her own feelings and disregards Mom's feelings.

"Well, what did you expect? What you did was so out of the ordinary" barked Grandma.

"What did you expect?" Grandma continues. "You had to expect this kind of reaction and by the way, what do you think my friends are going to say when they find out what you did?"

Instead of comfort Mom gets scolded like a child who has done something very wrong.

At first blush it's hard to follow Grandma's line of thinking. How could she be so cruel? I had to recall what Grandma told me in the interview earlier.

Grandma remembered a day in Detroit many years ago when she and Grandpa were out shopping in the upscale shopping district on Grand River Avenue. As they strolled from store to store enjoying a quiet Sunday afternoon, two black men that worked for Grandpa approached them.

"Hey, how ya doing, boss? Good to see ya boss." The men politely stated. Grandpa nodded to the men and continued on down the street. In this tiny moment Grandma was horrified. The white couples that they were with and the whites that passed by all gave Grandma and Grandpa disgusted looks because they were interacting with these black men. Grandma who envisioned herself a socialite was devastated by this incident that lasted less than three seconds.

If that exchange mortified Grandma, it was easy to see how having one of "them" in her family would be troubling.

In that conversation with Mom in 1968 I think part of Grandma was thinking, "How could my own daughter do this to me." Justified or not I came to understand how deeply Grandma was affected by my adoption.

The true depth of how she was affected came in one answer during our interview. I asked Grandma how she felt back then about her daughter adopting a biracial baby. I asked the question right after she told the hairdresser story and I received an answer I did not expect.

The emotions of the hairdresser story took Grandma back to that place and time. I could tell by the way she sounded, how she said it and that distant "I am not here look" she had. It was the purest and most honest answer I got all day. Quietly, Grandma answers, "I was heartbroken."

On my way home from our interview that answer bounced off the walls of my skull over and over again. The answer echoed again and again. I can still hear Grandma tell me my inclusion in to her family broke her heart.

Growing up I can never remember an incident when Grandma or Grandpa were harsh or rude to me. I can never remember an incident where their true thoughts bled through their Grandma and Grandpa façade.

Although as I sat behind the wheel contemplating our talk there was one incident that came back to me as I scanned through memories of years and years of interaction with Grandma and Grandpa. This incident was pulled from my memory and was in high definition.

Grandma and Grandpa were visiting us in Detroit. They would usually visit about once a year. Mom and Dad, my brothers James and Matthew, and I are picnicking in the park with Grandma and Grandpa. The orange and brown colored leaves that were painted in my memory told me the picnic was some time in the early Fall. The sun was bright and warming and I was watching James, Matthew and Grandpa wrestling in a mound of leaves. I was in my late adolescent/early teen years. Lisa, my sister, is not presents and I don't know why.

Watching Grandpa interact with my brothers on this fall day was like watching TV. I was watching it but not a part of it. I wasn't invited in and I remember feeling left out. They each pitched handfuls of leaves at each other and James and Matthew ganged up on Grandpa. They were laughing and screaming as the leaves floated the air. It was a scene Norman Rockwell would have coveted and I was not in it. I remember seeing their interaction and wondering why Grandpa and I never interacted that way. There was an easiness that their relationship had that I didn't have with Grandma or Grandpa.

This disconnect that I had with them seemed obvious that day. I didn't feel a bond with them as it appeared my brothers did. Watching them play together showed me a truth I didn't know how to handle. I was kept at a safe distance and never made it into that inner circle. At that time, the thought of an adult being wrong or doing wrong was foreign to me. So I concluded there was something about me that was unapproachable. There was something about me that caused that gap.

Since it was never what they did, but rather what they didn't do, I assumed the responsibility for what I saw as a fracture in our relationship. What they didn't do was treat me like *their* Grandchild. Instead I was treated like a friend of the family; it was like my adoption was never finalized.

On my car ride home from my interview with Grandma, I pieced together what I learned in the interview with this very clear picnic scene. The revelation that it was *not* me gave me momentary relief. The feeling of relief was followed with sadness as the gravity of this revelation slammed onto the top of my head.

I wonder if that is why Grandma and Grandpa only came around once a year. I wonder if Mom understood her parents and understood limited contact with them was best. I am sure now Mom and Dad saw what I couldn't see and had to answer the difficult question, "What do you do when family won't accept your family?"

This would be the first of a series of difficult questions Mom and Dad would have to contemplate.

The next difficult question they would have to answer was, "What do you do when the church won't accept your family?"

4

THE LUTHERAN INQUISITION

"THAT'S BULLSHIT!" My Dad, the associate Lutheran pastor responded.

A year before God placed me in my home on Monroe Street in Dearborn, Mom and Dad were making waves and losing friends in the church and the community. Living their faith, to them, meant acting upon what they studied in church. To Mom and Dad if all were not treated equally, part of their responsibility as Christians was to speak up for those who were not being treated fairly. One of the ways Mom and Dad did this was by protesting against unfair housing in Southeast Michigan.

Southeast Michigan had a history of supporting unfair housing practices. It was very difficult for blacks to purchase homes in certain areas during the '50's and '60's. Up until this time, Dearborn was considered a closed community. Non-whites were not welcome in Dearborn and the majority of the residents and the Mayor openly supported this position.

Mom and Dad felt these types of restrictions were unjust and immoral. They, along with several other people from the community, protested this inequality.

Unfortunately, the church where Dad worked didn't share in Mom and Dad's enthusiasm. Mom and Dad's extracurricular activities were seen by the church as causing problems were there was no problem. The church was made up of a large number of ex-Detroiters who fled Detroit to get away from the growing black population. Mom and Dad were fighting for the rights of blacks to be able to be live in any neighborhood they chose.

The problem the church saw with this was that it meant there was a potential that the neighbors they were trying to get away from in Detroit would follow them to Dearborn. My parents were tinkering with a machine that wasn't broken according to a large majority of the church. It is comforting to know Mom and Dad were outlaws *before* I arrived.

Mom and Dad knew their passion was met with hostility by the church but they continued to give time to a cause they felt needed their attention. Their ability to see all races as equal helps to explain why adding biracial to their list of potential adoptees was an easy one.

During the height of their protest, my adoption was approved and I was carried into the church. My presence was the weight that tipped the scales. Soon after my introduction to the church, during a staff meeting, the head pastor can no longer control is tongue.

"Did you adopt this boy to make a point and upset the church?" Dad's boss," the man of God," asks.

"Let me make sure I'm hearing you right. You think we adopted our son to upset the church?"

When Dad pauses to clarify the statement, his boss responds with silence.

The pastor sees nothing wrong with what he is implying. But he also knows to further explain himself may dig a hole he is not prepared to climb out of, so he says nothing. At this point, the meeting adjourns before a real argument begins.

The pastor's weak confrontation is a test to see how pliable Dad is. When Dad pushed back, the pastor's strategy changes. His frustration with Dad's actions causes the pastor to step up his attack.

The monthly meetings with the church council now become tense. The church council is the governing body of the local church. The council convenes on a monthly basis to discuss the direction of the church, their presence in the community, finances and events. Since my arrival another topic has been added to the meeting schedule. Over and over again, Dad is questioned about his job performance, or the way he did something or what he said, how he said it or where he said it and to whom he said it. Each meeting the council turns their attention to Dad and reviews what they were unhappy with and how Dad needs to change. It begins subtly with a simple comment and over the next few months Dad and his job performance dominate the council meetings.

Finally, Dad is standing on the end of his patience. It is painfully clear what is happening. Instead of pretending it isn't there, Dad walks up to the quiet elephant in the room and asks if this recent concern for his job has anything to do with racism.

Silence floods the room. The "r" word has been uttered and the council members respond in unison, with an offended tone, that racism has nothing to do with it. They just notice that recently *Dad* has changed.

The energy that has been put into avoiding the inevitable confrontation has exhausted the council and they call for a break.

During the break, Dad, who is still determined to get to the core of the council's issues, approaches a friend and council member.

"Ok, what is this really about?" Dad calmly asks his friend.

"They don't think you have the Holy Spirit," replies Dad's friend.

Dad is frozen by the gravity of what has been said. He knows now since their harassment didn't force him to quit, the council is changing their offensive strategy; they are moving to force him out.

The church by-laws state that although the council has the power to terminate a pastor, they have to base it on something. Dad knows that to be fired the council has to prove he qualifies for one of the following: He is a heretic, he is immoral, he is mentally incompetent, or he is lazy.

To accuse him of being without the Holy Spirit is a way of saying he is an unbeliever, or immoral. They not only have the power to terminate him, but if they can fire him by proving he is an unbeliever, it would make it very difficult for Dad to get work. Who is going to hire a Christian pastor who doesn't believe in God?

In an instant, Dad can see the council trying to grab from him his ability to make a living. In that moment, he sheds his clerical collar for his father's overalls. The rage and fear comes alive in his chest and fights their way out. From his lungs to his throat,

past his tongue, rage kicks open his lips and Dad responds,"
THAT'S BULLSHIT!"

The sound of the trap rings loudly as Dad steps into it. In that
moment of panic he gives the council what they are looking for.
What kind of pastor uses words like that? Only an immoral pastor
speaks like this.

It is a weak argument, but one that is worth pursuing the
council believes. To present a more convincing case the council
goes to work looking for another straw to grasp. They find it in
something Dad shared with the council in an earlier meeting.
Dad had presented an idea that he found in the Bible. The
early church in the Bible would meet in each other's homes, and
have what has become known as cell church groups. Although,
Biblically based and supported the council finds fault with it.
Their response is that this is an act of heresy. Only the communists
meet in cell groups. Pastor Hofmann is a heretic.

In this day and time, the fear of communism spreading
through the United States is a huge concern. If spun right this
provides a great way to get rid of a pastor.

"SNAP!"

Now the council must act. They have an immoral heretic
living among them and he must be extracted.

The next step in terminating a pastor is to call a meeting of
the church members and openly charge the pastor. The church
then votes on whether a motion is passed to terminate the pastor.
The council moves at the speed of sound and the meeting is put
on the church schedule. The acting Bishop is called and must
preside over the meeting.

One Sunday, in the middle of the afternoon the meeting
begins. It is standing room only as over 600 people attend the
meeting. Several community people who know Dad and Mom
attend to give their support, but the majority of people are here
to see the end of Dad's career. The chance to view a real life
hanging generates more interest than a Christmas or Easter
service.

The meeting is called to order and the charges are presented.
One member after another gets up and tells why they feel Dad is
not fit to be a pastor. Dad sits at the front of the church, not able
to respond to his accusers. Point after point is made.

"He's a communist."

"He is immoral."

"He lacks the Holy Spirit."

Anyone is free to stand up and say whatever is on his or her mind and Dad can't debate him or her.

Those that agree with what Dad is trying to do say nothing. They know to speak up in support would mean grave consequences for them in the community and that could affect *their* job or family. Silence brings security.

Punch after punch is thrown and Dad absorbs them. To the gut, to the jaw, to the head and he stands defenseless. This torture goes on for three hours and it is obvious certain people are given scripted things to say.

The wording and timing of each comment is orchestrated. As Dad stands against the ropes barely able to breathe, the council member, who is no longer Dad's friend, stands to speak. His role is to tap the last nail into Dad's coffin.

"Pastor Hofmann is immoral!" The council member says loudly. "He… he said..," (He pauses, as if unsure if he can say "bullshit" in church) and then bravely continues, "He...said… bullshit!"

The church is still. The whispering chorus that has filled the sanctuary for the last three hours stops.

A snicker cracks the silence. A chuckle escapes out of another member. Slowly, as the church digests what is said, the laughs join more laughs and rise to the church ceiling bouncing back and forth

A grown man just stood up in front of 600 people to tattle on another grown man for saying a naughty word.

Dad laughs, at first, then embarrassment rises in him. He is embarrassed that he has let his temper put him in this position. Dad knew this was not the way a pastor should act.

As the laughs continue and the tension of the day is finally broken, Dad motions the Bishop over for a side bar. The Bishop comes over and Dad quietly says, "Maybe I should just resign." Looking back at Dad, the Bishop quietly responds, "Not here, not now." The Bishop slowly returns to his seat.

The church is quiet. The inquisition rests. All eyes shift to the Bishop.

He rises to address the congregation. Standard procedure says he must now call for a vote. It is no secret. Once put to a vote we will lose. The majority of our supporters are not members of our church. Our supporters come from other churches so they don't get to cast a vote.

The Bishop calmly and decisively changes our future. He begins with a recommendation. The kind of recommendation a parent often gives a child; a recommendation that leaves no room for discussion.

The Bishop urges the church to go back to their small committees and talk. Talk about the elephant that is roaming the aisles of the church.

"I urge you to discuss the real issues that were raised in this meeting."

He quietly puts the issues on the table; the issues that everyone spent the last three hours ignoring.

Then he is done. He never puts it to a vote and no one openly objects.

We remain at the church for another three years with the Bishop's support. The council meetings revert to being more about the church and less about Dad. Life is more tolerable for a season.

Dad and Mom still endure constant insensitive remarks from church members but by now Mom and Dad have generated thick skin to insulate them from such ignorance. They grow to accept that the mothers in the church nursery refer to me as the "snotty nosed black kid." Mom and Dad learn to tolerate the obsession that many have with the fear that when I grow up I might date their daughters. Over and over again Mom and Dad are approached by concerned parents who ask, "Who do you think he will date when he grows up?"

I can't even pee standing up at this point, but several people are very interested in where my penis will end up.

Mom and Dad turn the other cheek. When Mom takes the kids to the local department store to get pictures and the photographer asks if Mom wants the "welfare baby" in the pictures, we never get the picture taken.

Mom and Dad stay to help create change but after three long years they wonder if this constant pressure will change them. They have no other cheeks to offer.

Grandma's words resonate, as a tough decision must now be made. "What did you expect? What you did was so out of the ordinary." Grandma was right. The decision Mom and Dad made to adopt me was extraordinary, not in a heroic sort of way but in an "out of the ordinary" way. This one decision would usher in the need to make some decisions that were extraordinary, not in a heroic sort of way but in an "out of the ordinary" way. The decision to leave the white community of Dearborn and move to Detroit into a black community is an extraordinary one. The decision was made to move into a community where I could be around people like me. The hope was that the new community would be more open to our colorful family.

Dad accepts a Call to a church on the northwest side of Detroit. The church has a racially diverse congregation. The parsonage is located a few miles from the church in a neighborhood that is more black than white and the polar opposite of the Dearborn neighborhood.

This extraordinary decision is made mainly for the benefit of one and now the rest of the family will experience life as a minority.

5

IDENTITY

The six of us moved into a small three bedroom, one story home on Whitcomb Street on the Northwest side of Detroit. We move into Detroit as the whites continue to pour out of Detroit to the suburbs.

The church is a beautiful church. I often go into the sanctuary when no one else is there and Dad is back in his office working. The sanctuary is large and the rows and rows of pews are divided down the middle by a center aisle. The side aisles are both lined with large stained glass windows. In the middle of the day, I like to stroll down the center aisle as the sun illuminates the stained glass windows. The sun casts a colorful shadow across the pews and down on to the floor. The church is quiet and calm and peaceful. It is exactly how church should be.

The reception we receive from the church body is a warm one. This is not to say there aren't those who object to our family composition, they just aren't as open about it as the Dearborn group.

The racial tension in this mixed congregation is there and the church members struggle with accepting each other. This is a congregation that is quickly changing from white to black and the older whites struggle with losing "their" church.

Dad has to step up several times to counsel one of the prominent whites in the church. Dad explains calmly and patiently that it is improper to refer to blacks as "them people" especially in church meetings.

The neighborhood is a bigger challenge for our family. The three white kids in our family are the minority in the neighborhood. They don't receive the acceptance that I do. All the kids in our immediate area are black and they do a good job of making my siblings feel different.

Tony Herb lives directly across the street. He is the oldest of the kids and the leader of the neighborhood. He immediately adopts me as his little brother and calls me his "li'l nigger." It is a term he uses affectionately and I wear it with honor. Tony is the first friend I remember having. He was about 6 years older than me and my first role model. I wanted to be just like him and act like him. I am in awe of how he responds to every situation. He has a detachment from everything. Tony never lets anything affect him and his impenetrable swagger is something I covet. He is cool personified and the fact that he takes a liking to me makes me feel ten feet tall. Tony is the first to plant the seeds of my racial identity. He defines what black is to me.

Two doors down from us is the Davis family. The Davis' consist of Marcus, who is a few years older than me, and his two younger sisters. Soon after they moved in their father left the family, and his amazingly large porn collection, behind. The boys in the neighborhood spend hours admiring the "art." I join them because I don't want to be left out. My conscience tells me what we are doing isn't right, but my desire to be a part of this group is more powerful than doing what is right. Marcus's mother works more than she is home and the baby sitter struggles to keep up with us.

Fred Parker lives a block down and he is the gregarious chubby kid who has no middle name. Fred is also a few years older than me. The fact that he is missing a middle name strikes us as strange, so we decide to give him one. His middle name will be Puttintang. Its origin comes from the children's rhyme, "Puttintang's my name, ask me again I'll tell you the same."

Marcus and Fred teach me the art of the five-fingered discount at the local party store when I am seven. We make the trek to the store daily to purchase Mrs. Davis' King Sized Kools cigarettes. I am too scared to try the five-fingered discount, and they make fun of me because I will not join them. My desire to wrong has its limits. They are tough kids who seem drawn in by the street life.

They too have a swagger but it is miniature compared to Tony's. I still study them and imitate things about them too. Marcus and Fred help water the racial identity seed that Tony has planted.

We live next door to Sonya, who is my age. She lives with her grandparents, mother and her mother's older brother, who is about 15 to 20 years older than us. Sonya's father is never spoken of and I have never seen him. Her uncle comes and goes. He is there for a period and then he disappears for a time. At five, I wonder why someone so old still lives at home with his parents. He doesn't have a name; he is "Sonya's uncle." He isn't around enough to warrant a name.

Sonya is my first girlfriend and I am attracted to her chocolate colored skin. When I am not running after Tony, Marcus or Fred, I am with Sonya playing house or making mud pies. My friends tease me about my friendship with Sonya but as we get older I learn from my friends that friendships with girls are a cool thing to have.

One bright summer day I am playing with Sonya in her backyard making our famous mud pies. My back is to her screened in porch and I am busy pulling the twigs out of the mud pies to make them edible. Behind me I hear a strange noise. As I attempt to swing my body around to see what it is, I am knocked to the ground. The noise I heard was Sonya's dog, Trooper, jumping through one of the screens on the porch. In hyper speed he reaches me and jumps on my chest and knocks me to the ground. As I lay on my back, trying to piece together what has happened, Trooper is taking bites out of my stomach, left thigh and making his way to my "secrets." Suddenly, Trooper stops, jumps off of me and runs back inside the house through the screen he jumped out of in the bottom of the door. I lay in the dirt still trying to come up with what has happened. Sonya has sat there motionless the whole time. Her reaction time is just as bad as mine. She begins to cry as she looks down to see I am bleeding from my stomach and thigh. I look down and the site of blood rockets me to the present. The pain strikes me instantly a fraction of a second before I figure out I have been bitten. I jump up and run out of her yard, around the front of her house and into the front door of my house. Mom is in the kitchen making dinner and my screams interrupt the dinner preparation.

I am rushed to Sinai Hospital (which was about 200 yards away at the end our street) where I get a Tetanus shot and the nurses clean my wounds. The bites are not deep enough for stitches but it feels like he sunk his teeth in to my soul. After a few hours, I am released with a souvenir syringe, absent the needle, to use as a squirt gun.

For the next few weeks Mom makes me drop my pants to show all her friends my wounds. I repeatedly stand with my pants around my ankles and my Fruit of The Looms covering my last ounce of dignity, as each puncture mark gets pointed out. No more are my "secrets" a secret.

I never saw Trooper again after our one sided wrestling match. My afternoons seemed empty without him. I missed kicking at his face through the face, or throwing a tennis ball or dirt at him from the safety of my side of the fence. My friends said the reason why Trooper bit me was because Sonya's family used to feed him gunpowder to make him mean. I always thought it was because Trooper was just paying me back.

Life on Whitcomb Street creates my first memories of relationships outside of my family. The days were spent creating memories like the Trooper story and being a kid and enjoying the fact that I was surrounded by kids like me.

Other kids come and go in the neighborhood over the five years we live there. The Holmes family, the only all white family in the neighborhood, lives on the edge of an old folk's home. Mr. Holmes is the director of the home. Their house shares a large yard with the nursing home. The yard is several football fields wide and long. They also share the outdoor pool owned by the nursing home. We only swam in it a few times because we were afraid swimming in the pool would make us smell like old people. The Holmes children are not an accepted part of our group so I don't see them much. When they do come around, they play with us but are not a part of us. At the time I rationalize that this is because they don't live on the block. Looking back I am more convinced they were excluded because they were white.

Fat William is a temporary character that showed up on our street. He comes around primarily to play basketball. We have the only rim on the street so our backyard is very popular. Many times we return home from a trip to the store to find our backyard filled with tall teenagers–most of whom we don't even know. Fat William is very generous with our court. I don't know Fat William's last name and William is never said without Fat preceding it. Fat William annoys me. He is a "user." I don't connect with him because he is only after my stuff and not a relationship. I am relieved his status was only temporary.

One hot summer day, we pull up in our driveway after church and see Fat William high up in our backyard cherry tree. He is about 20 feet up and eating cherries right off the branches. Mom immediately yells for him to climb down. I am amazed at how agile Fat William is as I watch him disembark from the tree. He must have the mind of an engineer to know exactly which branches will support his 300 pound frame. As his last chubby foot touches the ground Mom passionately tells him not to return unless someone is home. Her passion can be heard four houses away. William exits the backyard unaffected by Mom's yelling. I stand by Mom with my ears still pinned back from her verbal assault. His bravado was pretty impressive to withstand Mom's lashing. Fat William never comes back; apparently he was more affected than I thought.

My best friend Tony lives with his mother and father. He is brought up to be very respectful of adults and I like that about him. He would have never gotten himself in the position that Fat William did. Tony knew if word got back to his mom that he was being disrespectful, life at the Herb household would be tough for Tony. He had his limits. Tony never participates in the potential life-ending games, like "five fingered discount" that Fred and Marcus do. Tony knew if he did, this could mean the end of his life if his parents found out. Tony was a balance of tough but respectful, confident but not mean.

These colorful characters and scenes painted my everyday life. In them, I chiseled out the beginnings of my identity. They helped define for me what it meant to be proud about being black. The pride that I absorbed from them would protect me later in life.

At the same time, the risks and cost to the rest of the family was monumental.

Life for my brothers, James and Matthew, on Whitcomb is tough. They are the only two white boys on the block. Lisa doesn't come out much to play. The street is dominated by boys and there are no girls her age so she stays inside most of the time. Occasionally, she catches me inside taking a break from the outside and she experiments with my hair. I become her life-sized doll. She attempts to braid my long hair a few times and even figures a way to put rollers in my head. After a night of sleeping on the metal hair rollers, exchanging pain for sleep, I opt out of Lisa's beauty school. She retires as my hairdresser and assumes the roll of my protector. If anyone messes with me, I know my big sister will take care of him or her. Tony assumes this role as well when Lisa isn't around.

James and Matthew are picked on for being the minority. James is more of a fighter so after awhile they leave him alone and take the path of least resistance. Matthew is often chased and terrorized. He routinely runs into the house in tears because one of the kids has threatened to kick his ass. I am the smallest of the kids we play with, but I never get those kinds of threats. I am part of the majority so the oppression that Matthew and James are subjected to doesn't seem as real to me.

The whole family becomes a target. It seems like a weekly occurrence to have an uninvited guest/thief in our home. The most disturbing burglary comes one Friday night.

Friday nights are family night and we usually make popcorn and watch our favorite show "The Brady Bunch." This Friday was no different. We finished watching "The Brady Bunch," and we were being tucked in to bed by Mom and Dad.

The episode we just finished watching was the one where the Brady's go on vacation to Hawaii and Peter finds an idol that he hangs around his neck. Peter is told by the island natives that the idol is cursed. While lying in bed with the idol around his neck he says sarcastically, "Bad luck, come and get me." Less than a second later the large wall hanging falls off the wall and just barely misses falling on Peter.

That night I imitated Peter and said the same words when I went to bed, "Bad luck come and get me." Bad luck showed up a few hours later

In the early morning hours, Mom heard a noise that wakes her up. She immediately woke Dad. Dad, caught half way between consciousness and a dream, rationalized it was probably Lisa going to the bathroom. Lisa's room is down the hall from their room. We boys share the basement which is sectioned off with paneling to divide the large basement.

Although Dad was satisfied with his answer, Mom was not. Mom persuaded Dad to go check it out. Dad checked on Lisa but she was sound asleep—until he woke her up. When he checked the front door it was unlocked. Dad assumed that he forgot to lock the door the night before. He relocked the front door and headed back to bed. On the way back to bed Dad noticed a light on in the back room that we used as a family room. Dad again assumed it was an oversight and walked back to shut the light off. As he entered the room, his eyes found the empty space where the family TV used to sit.

Instant confirmation! There was someone in the house and Dad wasn't sure if they were still there or not. Dad called the police then hurried to check on us boys. We were fine and alone. It appeared the noise Mom and Dad heard was the thief exiting out our front door. As they waited for the police, they surveyed the house and noticed the screen in the dining room was on the floor. This is where the robber entered our home.

The police arrived, checked out the house and the yard and took the report. Later that morning, someone knocked on the door. A stranger stood on the front porch holding Mom's purse. He found it while walking through the Peterson Park that sits at the end of our street. Mom's wallet was still in the purse but the money was gone.

This is the purse that Mom always put on the upholstered rocking chair by the side of their bed. She put it there the previous night, as always. Our guest came into my parent's room and took Mom's purse that sat just inches from her head. If the intruder wanted to they could have killed my parents that night.

Soon after that, on a Saturday night as we slept in our basement bedroom, I wake up to lights bouncing off the ceiling and walls. I hear shouting and yelling that sound like the voices are in the house. As my eyes focus I can see lights in our backyard through the basement windows. The Detroit Police are running through our backyard shining their flash lights in every corner. The neighbor saw someone in our yard and called the police. The police arrive and attack our backyard. They are shouting across the yard to each other as they check the yard and behind the garage. The visitor has exited our yard prior to the police's arrival.

The unwanted visits continue. Over Christmas vacation one year, Mom and Dad arrange a Christmas away from the chaos on Whitcomb. We spend part of the holiday in a cabin in the woods surrounded by white cold. The cabin is bare, but it is an inexpensive way to spend a vacation and rides down the hills on our toboggan make the bare cabin worth it. The hills seem like they start just outside heaven and end just above sea level.

We leave the dog at home and entrust the feeding to Tony. He comes in the house two to three times a day to feed the dog and let her out to go to the bathroom.

After several days of sledding, tobogganing, and family time, we leave the winter paradise to return to our dog and warm house. As we walk up the front walk, lying on the cement are several clothes hangers partially buried under the fresh snow. Each of us kids walks by the hangers and pauses to make sure what we see is correct. The thought of picking them up never bleeps across our radar. Mom bends down to pick up the hangers as Dad opens the front door to find the house is torn apart. There are clothes everywhere, furniture is turned over, and dresser drawers are all over the house. The TV is gone again! The house is in such a mess it is hard to recognize what is missing and what is just out of place.

The Police are called and they come, inspect the house, dust for fingerprints, and take a list of the missing items and leave. We never hear from the police again and all that is taken is chalked up as a loss.

The nights on Whitcomb Street are always unpredictable. I am not afraid, but I know anything can happen and often does. One night about 11:00 pm our phone rings; it is Tony's father. He speaks to Dad and lets Dad know he just saw two figures creep in to the space between our bushes and the large picture window in the front of the house. He explains to Dad that he has his shot gun pointed at the two shadows and he is standing on his front porch after loudly requesting that the two shadows, "freeze or I will blow your heads off." Dad steps out onto our porch and in the bushes, afraid to breathe in deeply, are our friends, Marcus and Frank.

They are scaling the house hoping to return to the bathroom window on the side of the house to get a glimpse of Lisa coming out of the shower. Just a few weeks ago Lisa came screaming out of the bathroom after seeing two sets of eyes peeping in the window.

Dad asks Mr. Herb to lower his shot gun. Marcus and Fred are sent home and told not to come back. Dad doesn't have the energy to call the police again.

It seems like the police know us by name as many times as we have to call them. Reflecting back on this time, I never recall seeing a police car at anyone else's house but ours. I never remember anyone saying anything about being robbed. As I became an adult and was able to do some reductive reasoning, it was easy to see who was robbing us. It had to have been our good friends. They knew our schedules, they knew when we went on vacation and they knew exactly where in the house we kept the TV. They knew all this because we told them.

These intruders, thieves, and terrorists were the people we called our friends. Fred, the friend we gave a middle name, Marcus, and some of their friends saw us as an easy target. They preyed on us and took advantage of us every chance they got. Dad would also tell me later he suspected Sonya's uncle participated in the free for all. I knew I didn't like "what's-his-name" for a reason.

I play these incidents back in my mind and I wonder if Tony was involved in this activity and I always conclude he wasn't. It may be my emotions answering that question- I'm not sure. I still hold on to the hope that I knew him and that he and Marcus and Fred were cut from a different cloth. It saddens me to even suspect my close friend but the opportunity was there and the tempting call of the city was powerful.

During the time when we caught Fred and Marcus sneaking around the house, my feelings for my friends never changed. They were the kids I played with everyday. They weren't bad kids, they just did something stupid. At eight years old my attraction to girls was not what theirs was so I couldn't really understand why they would do something so crazy. Life on Whitcomb, I know now, was chaotic. The constant risk that someone would and could break in and the harassment that my brothers endured made for a stressful life for my parents, I'm sure.

When the church became the object of a criminal's desire and someone broke into the church it was less personal but more disturbing. It really showed what a desperate time it was then. I remember walking through the church soon after the police left.

There was glass on the floor by the back door in the basement. The unwelcomed guest broke the long thin window alongside the back door and reached in and unlocked the door. Once in we think he went upstairs. At the top of the steps to the right was Dad's office. The door to the office was locked so he used the same method to gain entrance into the office. He broke the window on the side of the door and reached in and unlocked the door. This time when he broke the window he cut himself. It is easy to track where he went the rest of the time he was in the building because he left a trail of blood. It must have been a deep cut because the trail of blood was easy to follow with large circular dark red drops recording his path.

He went through the small lobby of the office to Dad's desk in his office. He used a letter opener to pry open the locked top drawer of the desk. Nothing was in it but papers. He rifled through the side drawers only to find more paper work and Dad's mouth wash. He exited the office and headed up the stairs to the sanctuary. He walked down the center aisle to the choir stand and the pulpit. Then he entered the small room off to the left of the altar where they usually prepared the communion. He found nothing in there and headed back down the center aisle and out of the sanctuary. From there he exited the church through the front double doors. He exited the church with nothing of value. What he took from me was priceless. After all the glass was swept up and the windows were repaired and the blood was mopped up, I returned to the sanctuary. During my peaceful walk in the sunlit sanctuary, I walked over to the choir stand. I looked down and in the wooden railing I saw a large red circle about the size of a dime. It is a drop of blood that seeped into the porous wood. The wood was stained and the blood drop would not come out. In my eight year old mind, this person who robbed churches was still there. He would always be there as long as the blood stain was there. He took from me my peaceful sanctuary. I never returned there alone.

Many years later I found out the peacefulness of the church was disturbed before the robbery. As the congregation became less white and more black, Dad felt as though many were questioning if he was qualified to lead a predominately black congregation. More and more he felt he was being questioned as to how he could understand the issues of this black congregation. This was a feeling Dad had that he had no concrete evidence of, but it was something that concerned him. Because everything around him was so black and white it caused Dad to think in a way he never had and he struggled with this being reality versus him being paranoid. Later in life I contract the same affliction.

Again, the family was caught between the races desperately looking for a place to fit in. At home we struggled with just blending in. At Dad's place of employment he felt the clock was ticking. As more whites left and more blacks came his fear of being less relevant became more real. In the neighborhood, we sat in the epicenter of the "kill or be killed" mentality. Our family was the slowest gazelle and lions that surrounded us feasted on us on a regular basis. To this point in my life I am color blind because being a part of the majority shows me no disadvantages. My family experiences what I don't and they are very color conscious. Life on Whitcomb was hard. I see that now, as I know a different way of life. In my adolescent years I did not see the struggle because that was the only way of life I knew. To me everyday life included break-ins and peeping Toms.

I sit here now and debate whether our situation was a "color thing" or a "life thing." In this neighborhood in Detroit the law was "you must strike first before life hits you." The break-ins were a combination of living out that rule and finding the easiest target to take advantage of. They saw us as easy. The question is did they see us as easy first or white. The treatment that my brothers experienced was a "color thing." They were targeted because they were different and reminded of that almost daily.

In the end, the balanced family life that Mom and Dad were searching for would not be found on Whitcomb Street. Whether it was a "color thing" or a "life thing," didn't matter. The desire to raise a family in a safer environment trumped the debate.

After five years, it was time to move on and God stepped in again to move the pieces on the playing board.

Our next move would show me a mirror image of the life I was living on Whitcomb.

The Bishop who had saved us once before was in need of a new assistant. In the summer of 1975, Dad received a Call to be the Assistant to the Bishop. It meant a huge promotion and a move away from Whitcomb, and public school. We gladly packed saying good-bye to the nighttime visitors and peeping Marcus and peeping Fred. We moved to an upper middle class neighborhood on the North West side of Detroit. The new neighborhood sat only three miles away from Whitcomb but the differences in the two neighborhoods made it seem like we moved to a different planet.

With the new job and new house came a new experience for me. I would now be the minority in a neighborhood that was happily white before I arrived. I broke the color barrier on our street and would learn a new way to navigate through life. The colorless world that I saw would become very colorful.

6

PROMOTED

The two thousand square foot house has a large yard with a basketball hoop, four bedrooms, a finished basement, 1 ½ baths and quiet. The street is lined with large elm trees that create a natural canopy. The house was in foreclosure and Mom and Dad bought it for $20,000.00. Everyone says that is a great deal but it means nothing to me. All I know is that $20,000.00 gets me a better life.

I stretch out on my bed in the upstairs bedroom I share with my brothers, James and Matthew. I still have roommates but at least we are above ground. I sit at the window that looks out on to the front yard and I am amazed at the quiet. Sometimes I sit with the window open on a warm summer night and watch nothing, or I watch the moths fly up into the street light that is at the end of our driveway. Matthew has Ernie Harwell on the radio calling the Detroit Tiger game and I breathe in calm.

We are only three miles away from the chaos we used to call home and it feels like another time zone. The pace of life here is different and the hour hands on the clock move slower. Life will be different here in ways I can't imagine.

It is September of 1975. I am eight years old and the change is exciting. As we unload boxes from the moving van, a.k.a. the family car, a neighbor from across the street stops over. She introduces herself as Julie Tenbusch. She explains she and her husband, John, also have a large family; three boys and one girl. Mrs. Tenbusch offers to pick us up from school the next day so Dad and Mom can have more time arranging the new house. It is a neighborly gesture to offer and just as neighborly to accept. It is even more neighborly to accept with the promise of sharing beer on the porch later in the week.

Mom and Mrs. Tenbusch would share a lot of Pabst Blue Ribbons on the Tenbusch's porch over the next several years.

The next day, we are told to watch for Mrs. Tenbusch, instead of Mom, in the school parking lot. As agreed, our ride is waiting when the school bell rings.

I am nervous about meeting the neighbors for the first time. I lift a cautious foot into their dark greenish brown Catalina. Mrs. Tenbusch is our driver and her warm smile makes the first step into the car much easier.

I peer in to the back seat and there sits four kids, three of which have the blondest hair I have ever seen, outside of Cindy from the Brady bunch. John has dark hair, he is the oldest, and he is the same age as Matthew, nine years old. Mike is the second oldest and he is six years old. Mollie is the only girl and next in line. She is four years old, and the baby, Joey is two years old.

John is the polite talkative one and talks the whole two-mile trip home. I listen and say nothing. Lisa, James and Matthew all join in on the conversation and I just smile. At eight years old I already know the inevitable conversation that will be had in the near future. The ride ends before the questions are asked and we all spill out of the car with homework and books in one arm.

I carry in one hand my paper bag from lunch which houses an apple Mom always sends with my lunch that I never eat. Later, I learn to throw the apple away after lunch instead of bringing it home just to be used again the next day.

I walk down the Tenbusch's driveway, across the street and up our new drive way. As I get closer to the large two story house, it keeps getting bigger and bigger and I keep feeling smaller and smaller. I walk through the front door in to the foyer. At the old house, our foyer was our dining room.

The dining room is to the left and the living room to the right. Through the dinning room you enter the kitchen that has a built in dishwasher and carpet. There is carpet in the kitchen something only rich people have I say to myself. Off the kitchen is a small dining area we call the breakfast nook. I have never heard of a nook or foyer prior to the new house.

Everything is new and big and exciting and scary and overwhelming and great. Soon after we arrive home there is a knock at the front door. It is Mike and John Tenbusch and they brought the whole neighborhood. There is a legion of boys around my age.

They all yell in to the house, "hey, you guys wanna play ditch it?"

"What is that?" Matthew responds.

John explains. "Ditch it," is a game where one team is "it" and they have to find and catch the other team. In "ditch it" hopping fences, running through neighbor's yards, and going over a block in each direction is within the rules.

My initial excitement begins to fade. No way is Mom going to let us go that far away from the house.

"Can we go play?" I cautiously ask.

"Yes, go ahead." Mom surprisingly says with a smile.

The peace that I feel is not only felt by me in this new neighborhood. Already Mom is agreeing to things she never would've in the old neighborhood. Before Mom can change her mind, Matthew and I run out the door.

We are introduced to all of the kids and it is time to choose teams. The standard is universal no matter what neighborhood you come from. We all stand in a circle and each puts one foot in the middle. Usually, the oldest kid is the one who kneels down and begins the rhyme touching each toe in the center of the circle.

"Ink, a bink, a bottle of ink, the cork fell out, and you stink." When he lands on your foot, you exit the circle. If we have ten kids the first five counted out are on one team.

The teams are divided and now we are ready to play. But Mark has to run home and change into his "fast" shoes.

As we wait the inevitable questions slowly come out.

"So he is your brother?" The question is asked to Matthew. For a brief moment, it is assumed I can not hear or see them looking at me.

"Yep," Matthew says without a pause.

The inhibitions present when adults are around are quickly shed in a group of young boys.

"How is he your brother?" They probe.

Again Matthew keeps the pace and immediately responds, "He's adopted."

"How come? What happened to his *real* Mom?" This is the next question from another curious boy.

"Because his mom could not take care of him so we adopted him." Matthew says leaving no room for questions. His answer tells them, this is how it is—period!

Matthew and I have been through this conversation before. We know our roles. He is the big brother. He answers the questions so I don't have to. I stay near by and just look down until it is over.

As I remember this line of questioning I see so many things wrong with this conversation but that is how it always went almost word for word. Being described as "adopted" has left an impression on me. Never able to be separated from the legal proceeding that said I was a part of the Hofmann family makes it hard to feel a part of the family. I grow up feeling like the son of Mom and Dad and brother of Lisa, James, and Matthew but described as adopted made it feel like my name was followed by an asterisk. Part of my identity became attached to the adoption because it was stated in the present tense, Kevin *is* adopted, instead of the past tense, Kevin *was* adopted. This was a tiny example of how adoption made be feel different when all I wanted to do was fit in. I didn't want special treatment I just didn't want to be treated differently.

The questions about my *real* mother sounded funny to me. In my head the only mother I knew was the one that adopted me. My birth mother was the one who gave me up for adoption. Again, in this small conversation that happened over and over again there were three parts of it that made me feel different and artificial. The first part is having the conservation in the first place. I know it is necessary but in my adolescent years it felt like they were asking, "why does he have three eyes." Immediately, I felt like I was a newly discovered creature. The second part was the, "he is adopted" part and the third part is the "real" mother investigation. I have grown to hate that feeling of being different or singled out.

The last exception I have to this conversation is the explanation as to why I was adopted. The standard answer that was always given was that my birth mother couldn't take care of me. It is an answer to a question that provides no information. Many years later I would learn the real answer is we didn't know. This vague answer frustrates me because it provided no concrete answer as to why my birth mother gave me up. The true answer to this question is something I will search for over the next several years.

I have never known what, "not being adopted," feels like. The lack of continuity in skin color in our family never makes my adoption a secret.

There is no shame in being adopted. The initial conversation with a group of all white kids is uncomfortable because I am the only black kid. For the first time since I can remember, I am a minority outside of the house too. The safety of the majority is gone.

They conclude the question and answer session when Mark returns in his Chuck Taylors. I raise my head, the eyes turn away from me and we start the game. We don't quit until Mom's call for dinner rings through the neighborhood.

Being the "Jackie Robinson" of the neighborhood, I am the first black boy that most of the boys ever socialize with on a regular basis; it is a learning process for us all.

Peter Gallow, one of the older boys, refers to black people as "Colored" and he always follows it with a pause in the conversation, then he looks at me and says, "No offense." I immediately learn that you can say anything offensive as long as you follow it with, "No offense."

Referring to black people as "Colored" is not what offends me. It is the awkward pause and singling me out that offends me. It is a constant reminder that I am different; I am not one of the group. This is the biggest change from the old neighborhood. Now I have to accept I am the different one and am reminded of this often. I quickly learn who in the group may say something that will single me out. When those friends are present I am tense. I contract my stomach muscles in anticipation of the verbal body blow. It's never certain whether or not in the middle of a conversation they may say something that draws all eyes to me. Peter is one of those people. I am confused about friends like Peter. I do consider them my friends. I look up to Peter because he is very charismatic and likeable. I want to be his friend and I want him to like me but some of his characteristics I hate. Unconsciously, when he is around I prepare myself for the "colored" reference. When it comes, I just want it to go by as quick as possible.

The conversation usually follows a similar script.

"Then this colored guy.....oh no offense....." Peter would say.

I respond by laughing or saying something like, "oh that's ok." Peter continues and the attention is quickly directed back to the conversation.

Reliving those conversations upsets me. They upset me because I gave Peter and people like him permission to refer to me in a degrading way. The color of the person's skin never had anything to do with the story. But the way this person was seen as different was very similar to how Grandma used, "They "and "them." It was a casual way of putting a person on a lower level. I understand now and partially understood then that Peter and those like him didn't do it to be mean. It wasn't an intended shot at me. I also understood it was a learned behavior from those older who taught Peter their believed hierarchy of the world. I was often curious as to what the conversations would be like in their homes when I was out of ear shot.

The Tenbuschs, the family who picked us up from school, are great at making me feel welcome and I never get that kind of awkward feeling when I am with them The only time, it was ever mentioned was soon after we moved in. Mike and I were walking down their basement steps and Mollie looked up at me from the basement and turns to her Mom and asks, "How come his skin is so brown?" Mrs. Tenbusch shoots back, "Mary Elizabeth!" (Mollie's full name.) That is the end of it. Mollie is a curious four year old, so this doesn't bother me and Mrs. Tenbusch's embarrassment and concern for my feelings lets me know this is a safe place to play. Not having to flex my stomach muscles in anticipation of something wrong being said is a luxury.

I spend a lot of time over at the Tenbusch's and soon I am treated like one of their kids. If I do something wrong, Mrs. Tenbusch lets me know. She yells at me like one of her own children and getting in trouble has never been so comforting.

Unfortunately, not everyone is so considerate of my feelings. To the right of the Tenbusch's lives the Galanos. They are one generation from Argentina. Jose, who is a year younger than me, is their only child. Jose does not like me. I was not sure why at first but soon it becomes very clear.

We played football on the front yards across several houses. One day, while playing football, my team was celebrating a touchdown. Jose, who was on the opposing team, walked towards me and quietly said "Up your nose with some panty hose, some black ones." The way he said it and the way he looked, lets me know the comment is more about color than panty hose. Even at eight years old, racism is very recognizable.

This type of racism surprises me. When I look at Jose, on this cool fall day, I notice he has kept his summer tan much longer than the other white kids. In fact, he maintains a tan throughout the whole year just like me. We are each a child of color but he is able to blend in better.

My response to his comment was quick. The training from my prior neighborhood shot through me like electricity and I lifted my middle finger. The violent presence of my middle finger caused Jose to dart in to his house and tell his father. I was standing on the football field as Mr. Galano called Peter over. The older man's eyes never leave me as he told Peter to straighten me out and goes back inside.

Peter politely explained I had to be careful what I do and say to Jose. Jose has the habit of running in and telling his parents about everything. This usually is followed by an irate Mr. Galano who appears at their front door. They scold the mean child that has hurt Jose's feelings and disappear back in to the house.

This mixed message causes me to question Jose's motivation. Is he just a spoiled only child or is it because I am black. This begins a change in thinking for me. In the old neighborhood, if someone didn't like me, since they were black, I never questioned if their dislike for me had to do with my skin color. In the new neighborhood, this questioning of motivations appears and takes up residence in my head.

Incidents like this with Jose happen over and over and over. I am not the only one who is targeted so I flop back and forth between possible reasons for this extra attention.

Over the next few years, through our own socialization we kids learn to work things out. We all learn to live with each other and negotiate how to interact. Gradually, I move away from being the "colored kid" to being "Kevin."

As kids we still fight over who is out at home, who fouls who, who cheats at what game, and who is the best player on the Detroit Tigers, Sweet Lou Whittaker or Alan Trammell. But these fights last only as long as it takes us to come up with another debate.

Many times back then as us kids learned through our interactions, I would look up and see Mom's glasses in the dining room window. I thought that she was only watching us play. Now I know she was watching to see how I was doing in this new environment. She and Dad made another extreme choice moving us to this new neighborhood and she was making sure I was doing all right. Youth has a way of working things out.

Because we were young and our prejudices were not deeply rooted yet, we found out they were reversible. I also learned the prejudices that had been fertilized and watered for many years were almost impossible to reverse. Mr. Galano held on to his conditioning and he had a hard time accepting me into the community.

One summer evening, the summer of my tenth birthday, Mr. Galano came over to speak to Dad. I answered the door and Mr. Galano told me to get my Dad.

The thought of Mr. Galano at our door made my stomach feel funny; something was wrong. I went to get my Dad and then vanished into in to my room and picked up the closest toy to distract myself. The escape that I got through my imagination was shattered when I heard Dad yelling.

"If you don't get off my porch, I am going to put my fist through your face." The bass in Dad's voice scared me.

Mr. Galano decided to keep his face whole and walked back home.

Later, James told me they were fighting over me. Mr. Galano came over to tell Dad that someone had keyed his car and since I was the newest and darkest kid on the block it had to have been me. Dad took exception to that.

That next winter, early on a Saturday morning, Mr. Galano has a stroke that leaves him paralyzed and unable to speak. Our parents are heartbroken and rush to assist Mrs. Galano in any way. Mrs. Tenbusch is a nurse so her medical expertise and care is comforting to Mrs. Galano. Mom sends over dinners to be re-heated when they need them. Jose is swallowed up by the commotion and I don't see him again until summer.

I lie awake many nights wondering if it was my prayers to God asking him to take care of Mr. Galano that caused this to happen. The relief that Mr. Galano will not be behind his front door waiting for me to make a mistake brings me peace. The relief that I feel causes me to feel guilty because I have gained my relief at the expense of another family losing their father and husband, as they once knew him. Relief and guilt wrestle in my chest night after night. Eventually, I train myself not to think about what has taken place and the cost of it.

The summer of my eleventh birthday, Jose returns to playing outside with us. Surprisingly, he asks his mom if Mike and I can come over and play. Mrs. Galano allows me to come into her home for the first time. She is friendly and kind. She offers us cookies but I am not comfortable enough to accept so I politely decline.

After that initial visit, I come over more and more. Mrs. Galano softens towards me. I am not sure if it is because of what happened to Mr. Galano or because he is unable to object to me. I also ponder the fact that it might be because I wasn't the monster she expected. Playing with her son she saw a black child as just a child.

The three of us, Mike, Jose, and I often play with Jose's Star Wars toys in the front room. Jose has the best, most recent and most expensive collection of all things Star Wars. Initially, a large part of the attraction to going over to Jose's house is his collection of toys. The more time we spend together allows me to see past the toys to a kid who is likeable. As I grow to like Jose more and more, the tragedy of what happened to his father becomes more real and adds to my guilt.

Spending time with Jose in his front room watching "The Three Stooges," and playing together fosters an unexpected friendship. This friendship blossoms while Mrs. Galano takes care of Mr. Galano in the next room as he lay in his hospital bed. As Luke and Darth Vader fight in the front room, I can hear

Mrs. Galano talking to Mr. Galano. He lay in a hospital bed behind a partition just past the dining room in their nook.

Jose asks me a few times to come see his Dad but I am terrified of all the machines and noises that come from behind that partition. I also know Mr. Galano does not realize I am in his house and it's better that way.

In the first three years of life on Shaftsbury the lessons I learned have lasted me a lifetime. I learned the training from Whitcomb Street saved me. At eight years old, I was proud of being black. I was secure enough to withstand the new experience of being treated differently because I was darker than everyone else. This pride and security was installed in me back on Whitcomb Street. What I learned about who I was and what it meant to be black came from those crazy friends on Whitcomb who looked like me. The training I got from Tony, Marcus and Fred insulated me from this cold environment. The hits I took initially from my new friends simply bounced off me. The ability to detach myself from the situation saved me. The blows that could have been fatal were instead only flesh wounds. I was able to return the next day revived. Because I returned day after day I was able to build life-long friendships with people who didn't like me much when I first moved in.

I still see Mom's glasses as she looked out of the dining room window. If I could talk to the frightened Mom now I would let her know I'm gonna be ok. I am ok because you made the extraordinary choice to move to Whitcomb Street first. If I had moved to the white neighborhood first without the training from Whitcomb I am certain I would not have faired as well.

I continued to grow and negotiate my place in this new community. Although some situations were foreign to me and I often had to blindly feel my way through, it didn't always mean foreign was always a bad thing. It was the pleasant surprises that come from these new experiences that made the expected struggles easier to digest.

7

UNCONDITIONAL ACCEPTANCE

Shaftsbury Street became the backbone of my childhood memories. I experienced a rich, amazing childhood and would never exchange it for Capone's lost treasure.

When I was 11 years old, I inherited my older brother James' paper route, and every summer morning I woke up at about 5:30 to go to work. I dressed with half an eye opened and roll down the steps and out the back door to the garage. The garage housed my red "Town & Country" wagon with the tall red wooden sides. For a while, Mike Tenbusch, who has become my closest and best friend, accompanies me on my route. Usually, I take Outer Drive, which is one street over, and Mike takes Shaftsbury Street.

I wake him up by going to the bushes below his second story bedroom window where there is a string hanging down. Each morning I grab the string and pull. The other end is tied to Mike's wrist. As Mike climbs into bed the night before he slips the string on.

It is too early for me to ring the doorbell and wake the family so this is the ingenious solution we devise. Later we ditched this idea when Mike becomes concerned that the string will get wrapped around his neck when he sleeps. Then in the morning when I come to pull it I will strangle him to death. Therefore, we create a new scheme that doesn't involve the possibility of death.

The new plan is much less complicated. I call his house and let the phone ring twice and hang up. If Mike hears it, he gets up, and joins me outside. Some days I do the route alone because Mike doesn't hear the phone ring. I suspect Mike hears it some days but opts for more sleep. He helps me for free, so I can't complain. Most days, Mike is walking out his front door at about the same time I am.

On these early mornings we meet up after we each do our assigned section and we walk back home. During the week we return to our own homes and go back to bed. We are usually asleep again by 7:00 am. At about 9:00am we wake up and the day is ours. Our parents work during the day so we are left to create whatever fun we want.

On Saturdays, we sleep in until 6:00 am, deliver the papers and both return to my house where Dad cooks, pancakes, waffles, or French toast for breakfast. Saturdays and summers are great on Shaftsbury street.

The days are spent playing outside all day. Each day is a different experience. Some days the kids in the neighborhood gather to play baseball. Home plate is Mike's front walk and the outfield is our front yard. We play over hand, moderate pitch with a tennis ball. If you hit it onto our roof, directly across the street, it is an automatic home run. My older brother, Matthew and Mike's older brother John hit several, Mike hits one and I never come close to the roof. Baseball will not be my ticket out of the middle class.

Usually we are able to gather enough bodies to cover every position. If we run short we play, "pitchers mound." This meant that if you hit the ball and the pitcher is on the mound with the ball before you make it to first base you were out. We have some games that would make the Detroit Tigers envious.

Some days we play whiffle ball or stick ball or we race on our bikes. Once we got the insane idea to play Evil Kneviel after watching him attempt a jump over some buses on "Wide World of Sports." We build a ramp out of a sheet of plywood Dad has laying around in the garage and some bricks the Tenbuschs have behind their garage. Mike is Evil Kneviel, our friend Jose, Mike's sister, Mollie, Mike's younger brother Joe, and I are the buses that Evil will jump. We lie down in front of the ramp and Mike gets on his bike. He starts two houses away and comes rocketing down the sidewalk. He hits the ramp perfectly and clears us all.

At this age, we never entertain what failure would have meant. John, Mike's older brother calculates it much better than we do; with one punch John urges Mike not to do it again. Mike takes John's advice.

Our summer days are filled with a lot of testosterone and very little common sense. One day we take the ladder from the Tenbusch garage up to their second story balcony. We use the ladder to get on to their roof and walk around. One wrong step and we could have a fast trip to the yard two stories below. Again, failure is never considered.

More idle time leaves us to create our own entertainment. Mike and I decide to play assassins one day. I borrow my brother, James' BB gun and from my parent's second story bedroom window we take aim at Jose and his friend standing across the street in Jose's driveway. I lift up the screen enough to slide the barrel of the gun out. Mike takes aim and shoots once as Jose is walking in the side door. We quickly retract the gun, close the screen and erase all evidence. Mike is sure he hits his target, but Jose and his friend never react, so I am sure he missed.

Later in the day, we move on to shooting at the next door neighbor's garage window from my balcony and spend the rest of the day doing things we know we shouldn't.

When it is time for Mike to go home for dinner, Mrs. Galano meets Mike as he walks up the steps to his front porch. She begins screaming at Mike for shooting one of Jay's friends with our bb gun. Mike holds to the code and instinctively denies any part in that. After about 30 seconds of screaming, Mrs. Tenbusch looks out the front door and calls Mike in for dinner, away from Mrs. Galano. Mrs. Tenbusch knows there is a strong possibility that Mike did what he is accused of but she simply has enough of Mrs. Galano yelling at her son, so she rescues him. She never asks Mike if we did it or not.

Our hot summer days are filled with swimming in our friend Peter's backyard pool and countless games of Marco Polo. We often go out to Southfield, a suburb of Detroit, where Mike's grandfather lives. His large property in Southfield is great for playing any game our imaginations can create. Mike's cousins, the Walton kids, live nearby and they join us in covering every foot of the several acre property. Every trip to Southfield includes a trip by Mike's Aunt Ruth and Aunt Theresa's small ranch home. They are old, gray and gentle.

The parade into their home is always the same. One by one the kids, John, Mike Mollie and Joe go over and kiss each aunt on the check. After my second visit, I am the last in the line and not sure how to greet them. Aunt Theresa reaches her worn hand out and grabs my hand and says, "Well, what are you waiting for? Where is my kiss?" I bend down and kiss her on the cheek as she sits in her chair in the living room. Aunt Ruth then looks at me and says, "Well, where is mine.?" I kiss her soft wrinkled cheek as well. From this day on they are "Aunt Theresa" and "Aunt Ruth" and I love going to see them. Again, I am welcome as part of the family and this helps me to walk taller.

Being seen as different and treated that way makes me feel different and walk different. I am very shy and quiet. Often times I just want to go unnoticed because then attention won't be drawn to me. Being around strange people in an all white environment makes me nervous. My stomach muscles stay tense waiting for someone to say an off color comment that will bring all eyes to me.

In this small ranch house in Southfield, I can exhale. It is another safety zone where I can just be a kid and color doesn't have to be involved.

The importance of being around people like the Tenbuschs, and Aunt Theresa and Aunt Ruth was paramount. They fed in to my self-esteem. The opportunity to be surrounded by people who build me up becomes just as important as containing my interaction with those people that chip away at me.

My Grandmother from my Dad's side does a beautiful job of building me up. My Dad's Mom is a remarkable German woman who seems be stolen from one of Mother Goose's fables. Grandma has a comforting thick German accent. She is one generation from Germany who settled in a German community in Cleveland. Visits with her are often and filled with baked goods, great German food, and no color.

When I sit next to Grandma on her couch, that she calls a Davenport, with the delicate doilies that are draped over the top of the couch, I feel connected to her. She treats me like my brothers and sister and makes me feel wonderfully normal.

Grandma knew what it was like to be treated differently. Her thick accent gave her away whenever she left her safe German community. She knew what it was like to be judged and discriminated against. Because of that experience, I think Grandma was sensitive to my experience. Legally, because of the adoption process I was her grandson. Emotionally, I felt like her grandson, no different than my brothers and sister.

When I look back on it, that statement is probably not true. Grandma showed some favoritism towards me. She paid a little extra attention to me and I always thought it was because I was the youngest. The most beautiful thing is it never occurred to me she was showing me extra attention because I was black.

My thinking while with Grandma never involved color. She gave me more than what I desired, as did Mrs. T, and Aunt Theresa and Aunt Ruth. They saw the need in me to be treated like everyone else. Extraordinary choices.

These safe zones created by these women and my family were imperative to my development. The inclusion of these wonderful people and experiences were just as important as containing the negative people and experiences. Slowly, I was discovering a balanced existence. The normal childhood games and experiences combined with loving people began to dissolve my struggle to fit in.

As the summers ended, I would go back to a different way of life that I would now have to incorporate into my new life.

8

ALLIES

The summers end with school shopping and I go back to my double life. I return to the private Lutheran grade school, which is pretty much all black, then after school I return to our white neighborhood.

At school, I learn to talk black to fit in with my black friends. For the most part, it works. I am not as smooth as most in my class but they accept me most of the time. Occasionally, one of my classmates will point out that I talk "proper." This is a polite way to say, I sound white. To this point, I have learned because I look black, I have to find a way to be accepted in the black community because there is no chance I will be included in the white community. Reality has shown me there is a huge gap between the black and white communities and if I fail to be accepted in to the black community, I will get swallowed up by the gap between the two races. Choosing a side becomes necessary.

Grade school is an interesting racial balancing act. As the whites are quickly leaving Detroit for the suburbs, schools like my school are quickly changing from a predominately white student body to a predominately black student body. The teachers do not change. They are all white and the change from teaching a predominately white student body to predominately black student body is not met with enthusiasm from all the teachers.

The school principle is Mr. Lawrence Schmidt. He is also the math teacher for the seventh and eighth grades and the meanest man I have ever met. Mr. Schmidt is an old school Christian who believes in corporal punishment more than he believes in Jesus.

It appears he is trapped in the middle of the color shift and no one bothered to send him the memo. He is caught overseeing a school he would rather not. His lack of patience for his black student body is obvious.

He and his wife, who also teaches at our school and their four kids, are a large part of the school. Mrs. Schmidt is much more accepting of their situation and does a better job of being comfortable around the colorful student body. She is likeable and I wonder how she tolerates Mr. Schmidt.

On many occasions Mr. Schmidt loses his temper and strikes a student with his bare hand or with the yardstick he keeps at his desk for just this purpose. In extreme situations he uses a one-inch thick cutting board to strike students as well. The stories of Mr. Schmidt and his quick hand are legendary. I never witness it but in a school of 300 students the stories travel quicker than the speed of light.

I do witness his explosive anger that he carries with him like a sacked lunch. He terrifies me, and the rest of the student body.

I know enough not to make direct eye contact with Mr. Schmidt when walking down the hall. He often stands outside his classroom, between classes, making sure there is no horseplay. I realize horseplay can endanger your life.

In my elementary mind something about him is not right. He seems to be in a constant state of anger. The way he speaks to us if we forget a homework assignment or fail a test is borderline abuse. Your grade or performance is never private and he shares his displeasure openly about how you perform in his class.

I dislike math, largely because of Mr. Schmidt. His verbal thrashing directed at me crushes my confidence and convinces me I will never do well when it comes to numbers. The fear of being ridiculed makes it so much harder to respond correctly when called upon in class.

One of Mr. Schmidt's requirements for math class is we have to take and pass a multiplication and division test. If we fail it we have to continue taking it until we pass. It seems I have taken this test 30 times and each time the stress of knowing that if I don't pass, I may witness the rage of Mr. Schmidt's hand, makes it even harder.

Now I must take it again. I study and study and I just don't get it. I go in and I take the test and I flunk it AGAIN!! Mr. Schmidt sends a note home that has to be signed by my parents that says something like, "Your son is an idiot and will never pass math." Realistically, the note probably says something like, "Your student has failed to pass the required math test. Please sign and return this note to verify you are aware of this." I am given the note and told to share it with my parents and I have every intention on doing so.

In my haste to drop my books at the front door and race out and play, I forgot about the note and also forget to have my parents sign it later that night. The trauma of the situation must have blocked it out of my mind. Terror and panic attack me seconds before math class the next morning when I realize the note is unsigned. The realization that an unsigned note could get me knocked to the floor sends a rush of blood to my heart. My heart rate triples in a second and I am sure everyone around me can hear my heart clanging against my rib cage. I call on God, Jesus, John the Baptist, and even Noah to help me out of this situation. I pray for a flood. I pray for the walls of the school to fall, and I pray for the seven plagues, but God ignores me.

When class starts, Mr. Schmidt asks those of us losers who failed yet again, to come up and give him our notes. Again, he didn't phrase it that way but that is how it is translated in my head. I freeze in my seat and pray that God would strike Mr. Schmidt with temporary blindness.

Nothing.

How about permanent blindness?

Still nothing.

God chooses not to grant my request and Mr. Schmidt calls me to his desk, "Mr. Hofmann, I need your note." Quietly and absent of any self esteem I reply, "I forgot it." I purposely stand on the opposite side of the desk out of reach. Mr. Schmidt slowly looks up from his desk and I see the blood rise up his neck in to his face, and into his forehead. He looks like a thermometer and I am convinced the mercury is going to explode out of the top of his head. He points to the door and tells me to go to the office and wait for him.

I do as I am told and terror races through my body, and I play the scenarios in my head of how I will dodge his smack. I sit in the office in the seat in front of the secretary's desk waiting for him to appear. After what seems like six long years, he enters the office, walks by me and into his office. He calls me in and tells me he is sending me home.

Fireworks go off in my head. The halleluiah chorus is playing after the fireworks finish and I am thanking God for hearing my prayers.

I turn around and begin walking out of his office. He barks at me, "Get your mother on the phone and tell her to come get you." I am prepared to walk the two miles home and happy about it but do as I am told.

I call Mom and she is furious. To my surprise, I'm not the target of her fury. She is confused and upset and knows how difficult Mr. Schmidt can be. I assume parents are also scared of Mr. Schmidt so I expect Mom to run out of her office at work to come get me. Instead, she demands that I put Mr. Schmidt on the phone. I give him the phone and go sit in the office chair in front of the secretary. Mr. Schmidt says very little in the conversation. He comes out of his office, his face red again, and he tells me to get back to class. It is over. Whatever voodoo Mom uses works. Mom beat the man who I thought was unbeatable. The rest of the day I stay a long arms length away from Mr. Schmidt.

When I get home later that evening I hear Mom tell Dad the story and she is still hot about it. "How asinine can you be? Kevin is struggling in math and your solution is to kick him out of school? Giving him *less* time in class? How does that help the problem?"

When she says it like that, it makes so much sense. Mom has a way of getting people to see things her way. She made Mr. Schmidt see how this equation wasn't adding up.

The most frustrating thing about Mr. Schmidt's reign of terror is that no one seems to do anything about him and his rage. We often complain to other teachers and they don't say much. They give us the "I know, I know" look and change the subject.

Mrs. Gearns, our seventh grade and English teacher is our only hope. She is our oasis. Mrs. Gearns is a thin wiry woman who dazzles us with her entertaining stories and engaging style. She is a kooky but kind soul.

During test time she sits behind her desk and when the room is quiet as we are all trying to recall our grammatical rules, she cuts the silence with a loud declaration, "Someone is thinking about cheating." She stands up, grabs her big wooden pointer and dramatically extends her arms and closes her eyes as if God himself is sending her a message. "Someone towards the back of the room is thinking about taking out some notes. Don't do it." I never cheat in her class. I am too afraid God will tell on me.

She inspires us to be better than life tells us we can be. Even more importantly she challenges Mr. Schmidt. She is our dragon slayer. Mrs. Gearns is willing to do what no other teacher will do; stand up to Mr. Schmidt.

Mr. Schmidt and Mrs. Gearns have a very tense relationship and it shows. He is the most hated teacher and she is the most beloved. I am sure he sees it as her siding with the enemy.

Often times, students stay after school to speak with Mrs. Gearns about what Mr. Schmidt has done to one of us. It becomes a regular routine. The student knocks on the door of the teacher's lounge. The door opens and the smoke billows out from the freshly lit cigarettes. Mrs. Gearns is summoned and she appears from behind the smoke to listen and console the upset student. The student usually pours his heart out to her telling her what evil Mr. Schmidt has done. She is our safe place to land and at the end of the conversation she usually says something like, "This will be addressed."

She rises from the short counseling session, hugs the frantic child, opens the door to the lounge and is swallowed up by the smoke. It is obvious she will have a discussion with Mr. Schmidt.

Mr. Schmidt is temporarily kinder and gentler immediately following this process.

It is here, among people like me, where I learn that sides are drawn. Under Mr. Schmidt's reign we bond. He becomes a symbol of "The White Man" that the black parents warn their black children about. We gather together, and we talk about whites. They are different from us and I am included in "us." It is here where the white in my blood dies off. I look black, even if on a lighter scale than most, and I am treated as black. My lighter skin does not win me any preference. As I choose the color of my uniform, I develop a sense of pride in my race. Being the underdog, up against a weighted system, I am proud of the strong team that drafted me.

We all teach each other to be leery of whites. Anything white is looked down upon. This lesson is learned in subtle ways. One such way is when I smuggle in a cassette that I taped of Steve Martin's, *A Wild and Crazy Guy* album. In the back of the room, during lunch, I play the tape on my portable yellow Panasonic tape recorder. Several huddle around and we listen to Steve Martin talk about sex and use bad language, both topics are forbidden but being taboo to us makes them more attractive. We all let out muffled laughs and hope the teacher doesn't come over and see what's so funny. One of my classmates break up the party when he says, "Man, that white guy ain't funny. Now Richard Pryor, he is funny." Everyone agrees and loses interest in Steve Martin. No one chooses to listen to the unfunny white guy.

This white guy is still funny to me. I learn to listen to him at home and only mention that to my white friends.

Each night I go home to my white family. In my mind they are not part of the oppressive whites that we talk about at school. The Tenbuschs also get a free pass.

Race is not talked about at home. We don't openly speak about the obvious and with my white friends we don't speak about race either. Mike, my best friend, and I ignore our different colors. Somewhere we learn talking about race with another race is uncomfortable and should be avoided. We tip toe around the fat elephant that takes up 80% of the room.

Then one day, Mike returns my portable yellow Panasonic tape recorder that I let him borrow. He borrowed it to practice a book report he had to give. He recorded himself practicing his oral report to see how long it was and to help himself memorize the report. The book was, *Roll of Thunder, Hear My Cry* by Mildred Taylor. It was about the Logan family, a black family in the rural south in the 1930s. The book depicts the prejudices that the Logan family endures because they are black in the rural south.

When Mike returned the recorder his cassette tape was still in it so I listened to his presentation. For the first time, I hear Mike talk about race as he describes the unfair the treatment of the Logan family. He is sympathetic and passionate about how wrong he thinks it was for the Logan's to be treated like they were only because they were black.

This recording gives me the excuse and courage to openly talk about race with my best friend. I make a point to bring up race and it seems Mike is relieved; the tension is broken. Our ideas and thoughts on race are similar. The lop-sided society we live in, we agree, favors whites. We talk from the same side of the table and Mike becomes an ally.

My life experiences continue to line up to help build a more confident me. I learn my racial identity and pride through osmosis. The kids that surround me in school feed me knowledge of the black experience and I eat it up. I learn from them the differences between the races and I learn of a culture I am not exposed to at home. In my crash course on culture I find a more secure me. This environment at school builds on my prior training from Whitcomb Street and I begin to settle in to who I am and how I fit in.

When I go home, I am now able to discuss what I feel and how I see things and Mike lends a sympathetic and understanding ear. As Mike and I discuss race relations, our friend, Jose often just sits and listens as we try and figure out how we fit into this system. The system that Jose was raised under is challenged and he seems to be aligning more with our perceptions than the perceptions passed down to him at home. More and more, I see the environment around me changing and my allies are beginning to out number my enemies.

Unfortunately, the enemies still existed.

9

UNDERCOVER

I sit at the end of the bench because that is where my talent has put me. Mom insists I go out for baseball because it will be good for me. I make it through most of the season and I am still looking for the good. I sit on the bench with an African kid who is worse than me and I find comfort in his inability. We are on the baseball team sponsored by the corner liquor store in a league organized by the local Catholic Parish. We don't have cool names like the Tigers, or the Indians, or the Astros. We go by the businesses that sponsor us. My team is Parklane Cork and Bottle. The uniforms are white with green piping and a baseball hat that is green in the front and white mesh in the back.

We are nearing the end of the season and I can't wait for this to be over. The coach is Mr. Shade, a mean white haired grouch who's the father of our pitcher Peter Shade. They are white and so is most of the league. The African (whose name I can't say), Gilbert, the Hispanic kid, and me are the only minorities on the team.

Practices are, at best, humiliating. The coach rockets fly balls off his bat to the less talented kids that play outfield. I chase more balls than I catch and coach gets to prove he still can hit a baseball. Each ball I miss is accompanied with some insult from coach about how bad my skills are and how I should play the ball.

"Hofmann, you gotta get under the ball to catch the ball." His tone is harsh and degrading and I am thinking, "If I get under the ball and miss the ball, I will get hit by the ball." I consciously choose insults over being beaned by the hard ball.

The games are an extreme extension of practice. Mr. Shade, doesn't let up even though family is present. I play two to three innings each game because the rules say I have to play. If the creators of this league had not put that rule in the rulebook, I would have had a permanent spot at the end of the bench. I play center field or right field or left field. This is usually the spot the African kid was playing when they pull him out and put me in.

The outfield is good for me. I have rationalized that the ball can't possibly be hit fast enough that I can't see it coming. This way I can either fake to go after it or move out of the way; whichever way I play it, I will not get hit. As each batter comes to the plate I go over in my mind what I should do with the ball once I miss it. If someone is on first and there is a fly ball I know to chase the ball, after it gets past me, and throw it to second. I have gleaned that through the coach's insults at practice.

Batting is a nightmare I hate to repeat. I am a small kid and I fear that ball as if it is wrapped in death. At 12 years old, some of the pitchers in this league could throw this rock hard ball through a barn door. At this age, unfortunately the strength is there, but finding that barn door isn't always easy for some pitchers.

I bat near the end of the lineup. This means, all the good kids have batted. The African kid bats before me and the skinny white kid who stands two feet from home plate when he bats, bats after me. No matter what the combination this group of three is not going to start a rally. There is really no incentive for me to hit the ball. If I don't hit the ball I can go back to my comfortable seat on the bench–at the end.

The African kid is a magnet and it never seems to fail. He gets up to the plate, stands motionless as the pitcher whizzes two strikes by him. I say to myself: "He is 2/3 of the way; one more and he can sit down in one piece." On the third pitch, I look away. I can't watch. I have seen it too many times before. I am praying the next sound I hear is "Strike three" but instead I hear, "thud," followed by a gasp from the crowd, followed by a second of silence, followed by a faint whimper. The African kid takes the ball on his left side between his seventh and eighth rib. He limps down to first base, and as he passes by our bench, coach yells to him "Toughen up, shake it off!"

I force myself to take one step after the other towards home plate to go bat. My mind is fractured. When I get to home I look down at first base and the African kid's face is painted with his tears that are still flowing. I don't want to be him. I stand at the plate and concentrate on the ball. My eyes are glued to the ball so I know where it is and how to get out of its way. The bat rests on my shoulder. There is no way I can swing the bat and concentrate on the ball. I stand immobile waiting for 3 strikes or four balls. I will let fate decide what happens. No movement will be generated by me unless the ball is coming towards me. If it does come towards me, I may scale the backstop to get away. The pitcher sends three accurate balls my way and I am called out and relieved.

Dad loves baseball. He is a big Cleveland Indians and Detroit Tigers fan. I am sure my skills disappoint him. He decides being an umpire in my league would be a good way to get involved in my baseball career. The daily insults and relentless pounding of my self-esteem are not enough. During the season, Dad umps several games including a few of mine. I do find that Dad and I have a lot in common when it comes to baseball. As bad as I am as a player Dad matches that with his umpire ability. I can now see how painful it must be for Dad to watch me play because when I watch Dad ump; I get a queasy feeling in the pit of my stomach right about where it joins my intestine.

When Dad umps the games I am playing in, I get the genuine privilege of sitting on the bench with coach. The coach's son is pitching and we are in the field. As the coach's son hurls the ball past the other team straight down the center of the plate and exactly half way between the batter's knees and chest, Dad bellows out, "BALL." After three or four batters get gifts like this the coach erupts in to a symphony of words I am too young to say or hear, "Aw, you son of a bitch, that was a damn strike, damn blind ump." The coach is bright enough not to yell it. He says it just so only I and the other bench dwellers can hear him.

The coach doesn't see the resemblance between the white ump and the black scrub next to him. I sit silently praying a foul ball will veer off and knock me unconscious.

I make it through the season and unfortunately we make the playoffs and make it into the championship game. This only prolongs this never-ending season.

The night before the game Mike and I are outside playing and Mike suggests that I practice my fielding. We go over to Mr. Wright's lawn and Mike hits some grounders to me and tries to get me excited about the game. We don't even attempt batting practice. I do a decent job of fielding and the practice is called on account of darkness. I go to bed feeling prepared and hoping the sun will not rise.

The next day, I station myself at the end of the bench for the first 3 innings. Then after 3 innings I have to go to left field. The African kid comes out. I get no action in the field and I am excited that no one is hitting to me. I run in from left field after the end of the fifth inning. One more inning. The score is tied and I am just hoping someone ends this tie so we don't have to go into extra innings. We are batting close to the top of the order.

For the championship game coach changes the batting order. The coach decides today to spread out the three sure outs. The African kid, the skinny white kid, and I are broken up in the batting order. I bat sooner than usual today.

Our catcher gets up and hits a single. Gilbert, the Hispanic kid, gets up and hits a single. The coach's son gets up and hits a single. The bases are loaded. The next batter gets up and pops out. It is now the batter before me and then me. My knees are beginning to tremble and I am praying down heaven. I am pleading with God to let the batter before me hit into a double play. This season has been torturous enough. "Please dear God don't let me be the last out." The batter before me swings at three quick blurred pitches missing them all.

"Hofmann, you're up." Coach barks at me. The look of defeat mixed with anger consumes his face. I grab my helmet and bat and walk towards home plate. I get in position. This time I know that if I accept three strikes without attempting to hit the ball there is a good chance coach will kill me before I make it back to the bench.

I grip the bat tightly remembering to push my hands together. I have a bad habit of spacing out my hands when I hold the bat and coach doesn't like that at all. I dig my cheap red Beta Bullet gym shoes into the dirt because that's what baseball players do. I am still attempting to sell the idea that I am trying.

The pitcher winds up and zings a pitch at me. As it zooms towards me I realize his pitches seem a lot faster from this view. I wildly swing. I hit air. "Strike one." The catcher throws back the ball and I am determined not to swing at this next one. The pitcher flings it at me and I stand motionless. "Ball one." Now I am thinking, if I can get three more balls the potential winning run will be walked home. I can be the hero by just standing here. For once no action in a sport could be a good thing. I ready myself to not swing. The ball comes at me and I freeze. "Ball two." I am half way there. "Please God, please." The next pitch comes and I stick to the statute strategy. "Strike two."

"My God, my God, why have you forsaken me?" Now what do I do? I am panicking. Searching for a way out, but the pitcher already has the ball and he is winding up. This next pitch what do I do? Should I swing or freeze and I can't think fast enough and I am trying to figure it out as the ball is moving closer and closer and I don't have a solution yet. I concentrate on the ball watching it spin towards me faster than the speed of light and in slow motion. I have to decide. "Lord what do I do? Speak to me Lord." The ball is crossing the plate and I stick my bat out. It is a compromise between not swinging and swinging. The ball hits the bat and launches in to right field over the head of the chubby kid whose talent has put him there.

I run like my pants are on fire and the coach screams at me to run faster. I round first and head for second and everyone is yelling for me to keep going. I tag second and I stride for third. I land on third as the baseball lands in the infield. I stay on third and the crowd, my bench, my friends and my family go crazy. Three runs score and I stand on third. Emotions fill my chest and try to escape through my tear ducts. My smile stretches from ear to ear and I manage to damn up my tears.

I got it right.

The next batter hits me home and I return to the bench a hero. The next batter grounds out and our side retires. Peter Shade returns to the mound to end the game. He has pitched the whole game and is allowed to finish it. After one hit we get three straight outs. We win the championship game.

We cheer, scream, and yell for the next 5 minutes because that is the only way we know how to celebrate. Coach Shade cuts our celebration short as he out yells us all.

"Quiet down, quiet down we still have to give out the game ball. That was a great game, a tough game but we pulled it out and we could not have done it without... the excellent pitching of my son, Peter." He hands his son the game ball and says nothing to me.

Sometimes adults are just mean and it has nothing to do with what color I am.

10

TOUGH

Mike and I bond through our experiences together. I am sure people look at us strangely. Mike is tall, thin, and white. I am short and black.

Mike, his brothers, and sister, go to the neighborhood Catholic grade school. The Catholics are not immune to Detroit's racial shift; the color of their school is changing as well. Mike gravitates towards the black kids and develops the ability to talk just as black as I do. I still struggle with speaking proper, so we balance each other nicely. We are an odd pair but people get used to seeing us together.

Mrs. Tenbusch always says, "Whenever you two are together, there is always trouble." She means it in a negative sense but we take it as a compliment. Although we grow up in a quiet neighborhood, in the middle of Detroit, toughness is still important. We do not have much of it so we cling to any reference to us being tough with both hands. The depth of our toughness is measured one Friday evening in the middle of summer.

It is a peaceful Friday night in August just before dusk. It is still too early for the mosquitoes and the street lights but just after the sun disappears behind our house. We get the 'OK' to walk to the Dairy Queen. The DQ is on the corner of Six Mile and Outer Dr. It is two blocks up and one block over and this walk, absent parents, signifies the freedom of summer. This is the first summer we are trusted to make the walk alone. I am twelve and if I were as tough as I think I am, this privilege would have been granted much sooner.

Along with the freedom of going alone comes the absence of price restrictions. Before now, I always had to ask, "What's the limit?" The limit usually equates to a small cone. This summer, with my own money from my paper route, I can get anything I want on the menu. I already know that I am going to get a Peanut Buster Parfait. Mike will be getting the same. We have dared each other to step up to the window and proudly order "One penis buster parfait." If said correctly with a straight face, it can go unnoticed. If said incorrectly, with too much attention to the word, "penis," it is certain the teenage girl behind the sliding screen will catch it. Either way the thrill of being able to say "penis" out loud and in mixed company really makes us laugh.

Mike and I are the leaders of our small group of harmless kids. Mike is ten and tall, Jose is 11 and round. Mike's sister, Mollie is eight and quiet, and Joe is six and even quieter.

We slowly walk together enjoying each other's company as Jose, Mike and I constantly shoot insults between us. Mike and I have a connection that doesn't include Jose, but we bring him along for the entertainment value. Jose is often the butt of our jokes; sometimes he realizes it; most of the time he doesn't but he enjoys being a part of the group and laughs at himself.

The three of us start a game of B. B. Butcher. The rules are simple: anytime someone says a word with a "b" in it you get to punch him in the arm. The rules state you get to hit the person repeatedly until the one being hit yells out, "B.B. Butcher." The most skilled at the game can hit you so hard the pain takes your breath away to the point of not allowing you to get out "B. B. Butcher" at all. This translates into three or four extra hits. It is a thing of beauty to watch in the world of a 12-year-old boy.

This is shortly before Jose's Mom, Mrs. Galano, makes us stop because Jose is coming home with bruises up and down his arms. After the fun of punching Jay wears off, we talk about the girls we like in ways you can't when you are escorted by parents.

Mollie and Joe are two steps behind us and in a world apart from ours. We don't say much to them partly because we are forced to include them on our trip. It is a condition Mrs. Tenbusch insists on if Mike is allowed to go. We agree but ignore Mollie and Joe the whole time.

We all near the alley that separates the quiet residential neighborhood from the businesses on Six Mile Road. The alley is a buffer between the transmission shop on the corner and the small corner house with the nice lawn. There are different laws on each side of the alley. The neighborhood side is calm and friendly. The commercial side is chaotic and cold.

We cross over without even noticing. We continue our stroll and the new game of choice is talking about each other's mother.

"Man, Jose your mom is so stupid when the weather man says it's chilly out she runs outside with a spoon." Mike says to Jose. I convulse with laughter and Jose joins me.

"Awww, Mike that was a good one." Jose hollers back. Jose is always a good sport and appreciates creativity even if it involves his mother. Similar comments continue back and forth and no mother is immune.

We arrive at the DQ and we place our orders. Mike orders first, "Can I have a Penis Buster Par...fait?" He barely gets it out before we vibrate with laughter. Jose lets out a loud scream and laugh that comes straight from his round belly. Tears roll from my cheeks as I try to order the same thing. The girl behind the screen is not amused. She shoots us each a disgusted look, which makes it even funnier. Through his laughter Jay squeezes out his order and we roar with laughter again. We wait for Mollie and Joe to get their small vanilla cones and we stroll back home happy.

As we break from the large crowd that is lined up at the DQ, three boys about our age, ride up to us on their bikes. Their leader comes right to me, inches from my face and says, "Yo, man give me all your money." I recognize one of them from the neighborhood, but the leader and the other one I don't recognize. They are three black boys a little bigger than me but not very imposing or intimidating.

Instinct tells me to be calm, confident, and tough to have any chance at keeping my money. It is one of those things you learn as part of your Detroit education. Deep inside I chuckle because I know it is almost impossible to look tough eating out of a clear plastic parfait glass with a long red DQ spoon.

I give it a whirl, "Hellllll no," is my reply. The leader is insistent on getting our money. He demands it again in a harsher tone, "Give me all your damn money, man."

"Nah, man it took me two weeks to get this money." I say trying to sound unafraid.

We continue this exchange back and forth all the while we are still walking towards home. Instinct again speaks to me and tells me to keep moving.

Mike joins the negotiations by diplomatically telling them "No." Mike reasons with them stating, "Look dog, this is my little sister and you are scaring her. Why don't you just calm down and go away." I look at Mollie and I am convinced. Tears are filling her bottom eyelids and about to run over.

The three continue to follow us demanding our money and I continue to refuse to hand it over. Jose and Joe are quiet. Fear has spilled over from Mollie onto Joe. Jose is attentive but his emotion is easily read: he is scared too.

We have now made it back to the end of our street. I need to get across the alley where we will be safe. It is 100 yards away. If I just keep moving I can get us all there.

Mike is close by my side and I know if something happens I can count on him to help me. I am worried about Jose, Mollie and Joe. If these video game junkies start to throw fists these three are defenseless. We start to cut across the transmission repair shop parking lot at the end of our block. As we do, John, Mike's older brother catches up with us. I have no idea where he comes from, but his timing is perfect. John is a year older than me but is bigger then our three new friends. The three speed away immediately, so fast it is like they vaporize. John doesn't even realize the three thieves were trying to cause us harm. John is shocked when we explain to him what has taken place. From a distance the negotiations between us and the robbers looked friendly. John assumes since they have left we were safe to finish our walk home. John leaves us to go to Parklane Cork & Bottle to get some candy.

We are now 50 yards from safe ground. As soon as John leaves the three boys descend upon us. We continue our walk. This time the mood has changed. They present themselves only partially showing their faces. They shield their faces by pulling the collars of their T-shirts up over their mouths. This small change makes them more intimidating and they were more forceful with their demands. The friendly negotiations have been replaced with a hostile takeover.

They surround us and block us off with their bikes just a few feet from the alley. We are only steps away from the safe haven of our residential neighborhood, but we can't move without forcing a physical confrontation.

Mike and I only have prior experience fighting our older brothers. There are rules in fighting family members that I am sure these three won't adhere to. I can't see any way out. As I am trying to solve this problem, the leader reaches in to his shirt and announces, "If you don't give me your money by the time I count to 10, I'm gonna start shooting."

I'm not convinced he has a gun and his plea isn't forceful enough to sell me on it, but his acting convinces Mollie and Joe who begin to cry in unison. I want to hold onto the money, but more importantly, I want to hold onto my pride. Giving in to these three wanna-be crooks hurts, but hearing the scared cries of Mollie and Joe hurt more.

I reluctantly reach in to my pocket and give up the few dollars I have. Mike and Jose follow my lead and surrender their cash as does Mollie. Joe doesn't move and his size grants him immunity. The leader grabs the money from our hands and vanishes on his bike. His two flunkies stay long enough to apologize and shake our hands. It is a sign of respect and this gesture makes me feel better. They recognize we are not the punks they thought we were. There is honor among thieves.

We cross the alley and enter the calm of the neighborhood. Mike, Jose and I console Mollie and Joe. Their sobs disappear and are soon replaced with forced smiles as we try and make them laugh.

We all agree not to tell our parents what happened. Telling them what has happened will convince them that we should not walk to the DQ alone. We will become prisoners in our own neighborhood because of the actions of these three. When we get home, we sit outside on Mike's front porch and fantasize about what we would do if it happens again. We laugh and joke about how we would tear them apart. We joke about the 'tough guys" who got our money and all agree they weren't very tough. We make fun of each other and how each of us reacted and we enjoy the memories of the incident. This incident gives us "cool points." Since we survived the incident with only a few dollars lost, we are better for it. This incident will give us bragging rights in the future.

Jose gains respect for how he responds to the hold up. He passes his first real test. He is now someone we can depend on versus the liability we thought he might be. He has grown up from the tattletale he once was. Slowly, the challenges of Detroit begin to creep into our small community.

The color of the three perpetrators doesn't translate into evil in my mind. I hear the murmurs of the adults around me who flee to the suburbs to get away from the violence of Detroit. Often times this is translated into the whites leaving Detroit to get away from the blacks.

My mind doesn't equate black skin with evil. Fortunately, I see evil as actions and not skin color.

Shortly after the DQ incident, I accompany Mom to Grandland, a strip mall not too far from our house. It is located on Grand River near the Southfield freeway. It is a cold fall night. As we approach the grocery store to do the monthly shopping, a black man in his mid-twenties walks toward us. He seems to be walking unusually close which makes me notice him. He grabs the strap of my Mom's purse that is over her shoulder. He calmly but with authority says, "Gimme the purse, bitch" and he pushes off of Mom and sprints away with her purse.

We have a large family with three growing boys so food is a major part of our budget. The grocery money is in the bottom of that purse in cash. As I watch the thief streak away, I think to myself, "Wow that was quick, oh well, we won't be getting that back."

Mom thinks differently. She sprints after him, screaming, "Stop him, he stole my purse. Somebody stop him." I am pleading with my muscles to coordinate their efforts to allow me to stay with my Mom. She leaves me like I am running in cement shoes.

The purse snatcher dashes across Grand River, a busy five lane road to get away. All the attention of the parking lot is directed our way, including the attention of an off duty police officer whose wife is shopping in the grocery store. He and some others take off after the man with Mom's purse as he disappears into the neighborhood across Grand River. Soon we hear two gun shots.

Then silence.

After a few minutes, two policemen walk back across Grand River escorting the robber. The two shots we heard were warning shots that the police shot in the air. The audible warning stopped the robber cold and he surrendered.

The police officer escorts the robber back to the grocery store. We are inside with the police officer's wife. They bring him close to the door where I look out and see our robber. I notice he has a scar on his face. Mom is told she is not allowed to look at him because it may jeopardize the case. She will later need to go downtown and identify him in a line up. No one is watching me so I steal a peek out the store window and see the face of the robber. My eyes and brain memorize his face and the scar on his cheek. The scar makes him look meaner than I initially remember. I later share with Mom the information about the scar on his cheek, which helps her identify him in the line up. I feel good about being able to help.

This is different from the DQ robbery. The potential violence with the DQ robbery was manageable. A few punches and bruises was all I would receive from this incident. The risk was minimal and the threat matched the risk; all part of growing up boy.

The purse-snatching incident was more dark, threatening and sinister. The assailant was bigger and he sold the idea of being a bad guy better than the three DQ bandits. I did not let the purse-snatcher go so easy.

Over the next few weeks, eating is difficult. I know I have to eat but my stomach is in no mood for food. Sleeping is also impossible. I see the guy on the inside of my eyelids when I close them. The violent way he invaded my Mom's space flashes over and over. Fear takes up residence and my toughness deserts me.

Thankfully, logic doesn't desert me and I see these isolated incidents as incidents done by bad people not black people. My racial maturity allows me to distinguish between the two. My racial maturity also allows me to see less color more and more.

11

ANOTHER BROTHER

We grow older and the games of "ditch it" stop. The baseball games are replaced with whiffle ball only. Whiffle ball only requires three people, a batter, a pitcher and an outfielder. Peter and a lot of the other kids leave Detroit and move to the suburbs, so finding enough players for regular baseball is tough.

Matthew, who is a baseball fanatic, invents a game where the distance you hit the ball in the air determines your base. We play on Mr. Wright's lawn. His fence that separates the backyard from the front yard is our backstop. If you hit it from there to the sidewalk in the air it is a single. If you hit it in the street it is a double, the lawn across the street is a triple and the sidewalk across the street is a home run. Hitting a whiffle ball that distance is next to impossible. If there is any kind of wind the home run ball is impossible.

Running through the neighborhood is now too strenuous and not cool. The yearly block parties we used to have are less frequent.

The block parties would take place on a Saturday afternoon. Our block would be closed off to traffic and we would set up picnic tables in the street and play games and eat and socialize with our neighbors. They were one of the highlights of each summer.

Now the block parties are every other year and the games are for the younger kids. The last block party we all ever attend is the year we have a visit from the Detroit Police. A mounted police officer and his horse are commissioned to join our party.

Mike, James, Matthew, Jose and I sit around and watch as each kid is slowly paraded around on top of the horse. The officer in full uniform leads the horse up and down the street. We all joke about what we would do if we got on the horse and how we would make it take off at full speed. It is typical testosterone filled conversation. Gradually the talk turns into a challenge and Mike accepts. We dare him to ask to ride the horse and then make the horse run down the street away from the officer and the party.

Mike waits in line with the smaller kids. He towers over them and they are half his age. Mike gets to the front of the line and climbs on the horse. The officer asks Mike if he has ever ridden before and Mike confidently says "Yes." Mike is so convincing that the officer allows him to ride the horse without his assistance. The officer is tired of walking and is looking for a break, which Mike gladly provides.

Mike walks the horse slowly about ten yards. We are all on the ground laughing uncontrollably because Mike has conned this guy into trusting him. The ten yards turns into twenty and then it happens. I am not sure it is done on purpose or maybe something spooks the horse, but the horse goes from a walk to a full gallop in less than a second.

The horse is now 100 yards away and gaining speed. We all scream as Mike and the horse take a left at the end of the block and disappear. The horse is heading for Outer Drive which is a four lane roadway divided by a grass median. The speed limit on Outer Drive is 40 miles per hour and a collision with a car at this speed would most likely kill the horse and the equestrian.

Just before Mike disappears he is bouncing up and down on the horse and his long thin legs are flying up and down and kicking the horse with each bump, which just stirs the horse to go faster.

The Police officer watches as his partner sprints around the corner and out of sight. He frantically jumps into his truck and pursues his horse and Mike. The horse gallops across Outer Drive, somehow avoiding contact with the cars that speed down the street, and the horse continues on his journey carrying Mike along as a hostage.

Our joke has now turned to panic for everyone, including Mike who is atop of this horse with no idea of how to make it stop. As Mike passes stunned Detroiters walking down the street, he screams to them, "Hey, do you know how to make a horse stop?" He is never in ear shot long enough to hear an answer. Then suddenly, just as suddenly as the horse began, he slows down and stops. The officer catches up with them and takes back his horse and makes Mike walk home. The officer loads the horse into the trailer and never returns to our block party.

By this time we have all sprinted around the corner to see the Officer pull away and Mike walking towards us with a crazy smile. We all cheer as he walks up to us. Once in the safe fold of our group we all pat him on the back and give him a hero's welcome. It is an amazing way to end a block party.

Crazy stories like this continue to paint our memories and color has nothing to do with them.

Childhood games are replaced by all night basketball games in the Tenbusch backyard. As adolescence dissolves into our teenage years, we sit for hours and play horse, 21, sign out, or two on two.

The games of Mike and me, against our older brother's, John and Matthew, always end in a fight, which ends with Mike or I getting punched by our older brother. An older brother never takes losing to his younger brother well and it is becoming more and more frequent.

When we aren't playing basketball, we sit on the picnic table in the Tenbusch backyard and just talk. We sit for hours and talk about nothing. Jose joins us as Matthew and John disappear into the business of their teenage lives. Jose slowly becomes part of us instead of the kid we keep on the outside.

We talk about the girls and women we are attracted to and what we would like to do to them and Jose joins in with us. The crude conversation is always the same. Someone would say, "If you had a chance to sleep with anyone in the world whom would you choose?"

Anita Baker, Sade, Irene Cara, Lisa Bonet, Vanessa Williams, and the ladies from the rap group Salt and Pepa, are all likely candidates. The debates as to who looks better are endless.

We talk about girls we know from school and those that we all find attractive are all black. The color barriers we all grew up under are now gone. The three of us sit there hour after hour never realizing how far we have come. Jose's Dad still lies in the hospital bed in the house next door and it breaks my heart that my friend has to see his dad like this for so many years. The boy I used to hate has become another brother to me.

12

DIVERSITY TRAINING

The spring of 1981 brings a joyous and sad occasion. I graduate from grade school. The school where I am accepted and where everyone knows my story is now over for me. I move on to the local Catholic high school to start my high school career. My grade school classmates all go to the local Lutheran High School or to the public college prep high schools, Cass Tech or Renaissance High School. No one follows me

I carry 110 pounds on my small frame and I am shy and unsure of myself. The transition from the small grade school is not easy for me. I am used to a school with about 250 students and now I go to a school about four times that size. The high school is small, as far as high schools go, but it is a big change for me.

The first day of high school is tough. I was never the most fashion conscious so I always seem to pick the wrong kind of clothes to wear. School clothes shopping usually consists of going with Mom and letting Mom pick out the most clothes for the cheapest amount of money. This left no room for buying anything that is close to fashionable.

No one lets me in on the secret that most 14 years olds aren't comfortable with themselves yet, so I feel like I stick out instead of fit in. The tag of talking proper sticks with me, making me even more self-conscious. I say little to anyone and no one says anything to me. I miss the safe surroundings of grade school. I stand at my high school locker dialing over and over again the combination and I can't get my locker open, this only adds to the torture of my painful first day.

Walking home from school, I decide I won't be back again. Close to tears, I explain to Mom how my day was the worst day on earth–ever. Mom does not agree with my plan of not returning. It is not negotiable; I will go back the next day.

She assigns James to help me with my locker the next day and that begins a string of better days. Good days and bad days find me, and slowly I make friends. By the end of the year I am more comfortable. Having my brothers, James and Matthew there helps but also means I have to explain our family over and over. Fortunately, by now, I am used to it and it becomes a good icebreaker now that I am more comfortable with the one who was adopted. My story is unique and over the last few years this once uncomfortable conversation has become one that gets me positive attention.

Our high school was about 80% white when my sister, Lisa, started her freshman year five years ago. It is now the opposite and the shades of the school are changing fast. Once again, James and Matthew are part of the minority, and I am part of the majority, but with a larger population it is harder to hide my racial shortcomings.

My upbringing is different. I know little of the black traditions and culture compared to those that have lived it since birth, and in high school I get an education in what I don't know.

Initially, I hated to admit to my close friends my ignorance on things they know so intimately. Over time, these friends understand my upbringing and understand why I don't know certain things. I become more comfortable admitting I don't know people like Minnie Riperton, a celebrated female singer in the black community. I admit I have never seen movies like *Cooley High*, or *Shaft* and I have never tried chitterlings and don't even know what they are or where the come from. Initially, my friends are shocked but they remember I was raised by a pack of whites and they understand.

They do not alienate me or shun me and take time explaining things to me. Two of my closest friends tutor me in black culture and instruct me in many ways including dance.

Shortly before the homecoming dance my junior year, I divulge to Tyrone and Curt, my closest friends that I can't dance. This is after I have asked someone to go to the dance and we have all made plans to triple date in Curt's big Pontiac. Consideration was given to coming down with a cold, or cancer, or running away but I decided this was something I had to tackle.

The evolving social side of me really wants to go, if only we could have a non-dancing dance.

After my announcement, Tyrone responds, "You can't what?" He looks at me and the look of shame on my face causes him to back off. This is one stereotype I am so upset is not true. Rhythm was not attached to my genes. Instead, rhythms evil twin, "No body control what so ever," is what my genes are constructed of. Tyrone is determined to prove to me I am wrong and that he can make the dancer in me come alive. Curt and Tyrone hold dance lessons in my basement. We turn on my small radio, pop in a cassette tape and they attempt to teach me The Smurf and The German Smurf: the two dances every person of color can do from Utah to Ethiopia. It consists of coordinated movements between both arms and legs and my muscles go on strike. It appears the unions in my arms and the unions in my legs are in a dispute and refuse to work together. The end result is a huge work stoppage. Forcing it, even calling on scab workers to do the work in my arms and legs fails. After hours of teaching, Tyrone declares, I have no rhythm and surrenders.

The hope that I had at the beginning of the lesson is shattered. I understand Tyrone's frustration but his giving up on me stings a little. My pain is intensified when I share with Mike that I just couldn't get it and Mike proceeds to make his body do what mine refuses to do. The white guy can dance and I can't. What a cruel joke I am a part of. "My God, My God why hath thou forsaken me, again?"

Mom and I go out and purchase a new suit. The suit matches and is stylish. The tutoring is paying off. I spend $70.00 on a pair of black leather Roots; the most "in" shoes and I have a shot at pulling this thing off. Breaking a leg at this point would make my experience a success and help me avoid the dance snafu. Mom is appalled that the shoes cost more than the suit, but my paper route money is sacrificed for the shoes so she is unable to object. The night of the dance I am ready. Dancing will not be a part of my homecoming experience and explaining this to my date was a painful conversation. She agrees to still go because all her friends will be there. I am relieved and slightly wounded. It doesn't appear I figure into her homecoming plans.

I have my date's corsage and I am awaiting the arrival of Curt's maroon Pontiac to pull up in the driveway. We agree, he will pick up his date, then Tyrone and Tyrone's date, and then me and my date. Our plan fails immediately.

Curt is an hour late and out of touch. Calling his house number does nothing but ring and ring. Calling Tyrone only confirms Curt is AWOL. Watching out the dining room window, I am hoping my date doesn't call here again asking when I'm going to pick her up. The last time she called she advised if I don't show up soon she is going without me. As time clicks by it is more evident I am more of a chauffer than a date to my partner.

Finally, bright headlights shine in my eyes as a vehicle pulls up in our driveway. It is not the vehicle I expect. Instead, it is Curt's father's Transvan. The Transvan is a large van, bigger than a conversion van, with the amenities of a motor home. It has a couch, a dining room table and plenty of room. It will make the two mile trip to the dance much more comfortable. The initial plan was to fit four in the back seat of the Pontiac, which would have been a tight but welcomed squeeze on my first official date.

Curt explains the Pontiac refuses to turn over and he has spent the last two hours praying over it. Curt is a motor head and if he can't get it to run Jesus himself can't bring it back to life.

I sprint to the phone to catch my date before her angry mother takes her to the dance. After a quick conversation that involves a lot of phases like, "I am so sorry," and "Please forgive me," I sprint to the Transvan to pick up my date.

My date is the most uptight of the group. She is a sophomore and it is also her first date. After calling her mother three weeks ago and asking her mother if she could go; begging and pleading with her mother, she was given the green light to go. It is clear her mother doesn't like me much but this is her daughter's first date so she puts up with her daughter's ill-advised choice in dates. The tardiness of the night doesn't make me more likeable and it is not helping me dig out of my unjust hole.

On the way to her house, it occurs to us all that driving up in front of her house in a vehicle perfectly suited for making babies, is not going to make my trek out of the hole any easier. It is a funny scenario until we pull up to her house.

I jump out and go to her door, and explain the situation. Her mother is not pleased but because we are so late she agrees to let her daughter go. The new suit, shoes, and corsage are what tip the scales I am sure.

We arrive at the dance late, which works out great for me. We have less time to dance and I am ok with that. After standing on the wall with my date watching everyone else dance, the song, *Angel* by Anita Baker pumps out through the large speakers and my date twitches and she can't stand still.

"Oh this is my song." She says and looks at me. Since the music is so loud I pretend I can't hear her. We are not close enough as a couple for me to risk the embarrassment of getting on the dance floor. She turns to find someone else to dance with and I am relieved.

The dance or non-dance is finally over. I have survived without getting on the dance floor and I am so happy. My date doesn't share my enthusiasm.

We all hang around and talk to friends and then make our way back to the Transvan. As we are walking, Jimmy Jam, a fellow track and cross country team mate who is the best dancer in the school notices my Roots.

"Hof, are you wearing Roots?"

I smile slightly and calmly and say, "Yeah."

"Nice shoes, Hof."

My reputation of being below average in the fashion department makes this a surprising and shocking sight to my friends. Inside I am busting. This night has been great no matter what my date thinks.

We break up soon after the dance after some female friends convince me I can do better. More and more I am becoming more comfortable with myself. Finding my way and how I am most comfortable is a journey with a reachable destination.

The difference in food between my house and Curt and Tyrone's house is shocking. One night while hanging out at Curt's house his mother asks if I would like to stay for dinner. Over the past 30 minutes I have sat in their kitchen and watched the aroma rise from the stove and create a tornado of smells and steam twisting and turning and spinning together. The tornado converges on my nose and a waterfall of saliva forms in my mouth.

I reply, "Thank you, yes I must stay… I mean I would love to stay for dinner."

Curt's mom is making pepper steak, home made rolls, potatoes, sickening sweet red Kool-aid and peach cobbler for dessert. I lean over and ask Curt who else is coming to dinner and what is the special occasion. Curt laughs and tells me his mom cooks like this all the time. She sets all the food out and it looks like a spread for a platoon.

Dinner is served and I don't know where to begin. If I could climb in this plate and bathe in this flavor I would. The food is spicy, hot, sharp, tender, and perfect. My mouth feels like it is crying, sobbing, balling, drooling for another forkful. The plate has my undivided attention and I completely block out the conversation around me. All my senses are directed toward the end of my fork. I eat until I can't eat any more. I consider going into the bathroom and trying to make myself puke to create more room for more food. I decide against it because I am a loud puker and they will hear what I am doing.

The differences in my house and Curt and Tyrone's houses are interesting. It sparks an interest in me that I carry for years. The differences in cultures fascinate me and I enjoy pointing them out. Faulting my parents for not going to school to learn how to cook like a black woman from the south is not a thought that invades my head. Yet, what I lack culturally, although it is no one's fault, does create a small void in me.

Music is another area that is vastly different in my household versus those I go to school with. Growing up, the music we listened to was what Mom and Dad enjoyed. Simon and Garfunkel, Peter, Paul and Mary, the soundtrack to Westside Story, the soundtracks to Jesus Christ Superstar and Godspell, the music of George Gershwin, and Arthur Fiedler and The Boston Pops. Outside our front door on Whitcomb Street the sounds of Motown dominated the air. The Jackson Five, The Temptations, The Four Tops, Marvin Gaye, Barry White, and Aretha Franklin are what my black friends listened to in their homes.

As I get older, The Soundtrack from Annie, Classical music and ABBA are in our record player. Michael Jackson, Prince, The Time, and Run DMC are artists I share with my friends. I would never admit it publicly, but I like it all.

Mom and Dad take it too far when they drag us to Orchestra Concerts. I would sit in the large theater at The Detroit Institute of Arts and wish for a national emergency so I wouldn't have to sit through two hours of torture. To pass the time, at one concert, (they took us to several) I hurl penny after penny into the crowd when Mom is lost in the music and not paying attention to what I am doing. *Peter and the Wolf* has never been so violent.

The dawning of my own interest in music really begins in the sixth grade. Stevie Wonder is adopted as my favorite artist. In school I am introduced to Stevie's song, *Sir Duke* from his album, *Songs in the Key of Life.* I fall in love with the horns in this song and Stevie inspires me. He becomes a hero of mine and in music class when we have to pick a musician for a report I greedily snatch up Stevie Wonder. I go to the library and I research anything and everything about Stevie. The report also has to include a song of the artist we chose. Mom purchases the entire album, which isn't cheap. It is a double album plus a bonus 45 record.

Mom and I sit in the living room and put on the album and we listen to Stevie together. I get lost in Stevie's poetry and his amazing blend of instruments. Mom likes how he speaks about injustice and is so politically aware. This is a special time for me to sit on our old brown couch listening to Stevie and sharing him with Mom. The music may not be her favorite, but the message and the fact that I like it means a lot to her. In this music filled afternoon, I learn it is all right to express myself and find my own way. It is an afternoon that will never depart from my memory.

Music becomes a way to express myself and a way to bond to my culture. I am drawn to black artists, mostly R & B and rap. Becoming more aware of music helps me to assimilate with my peers. It is not forced or fake, it is what I grow to like. Having more in common with my peers makes me feel more a part of them. My only problem is that Stevie is my ground zero. The history of black music before Stevie isn't in my memory bank like it is with the black friends who grew up with it.

The loss of a culture is one of the things I grieve as a result of being adopted.

High school becomes a great training ground for learning how to socialize. I join the track team my freshman year and run all four years. I join the cross country team my sophomore year and run cross country my junior and seniors years as well. Being a part of a team and getting to know people I otherwise wouldn't is a wonderful way for me to show others I am more than just the quiet, shy, little light skinned boy.

Matthew also runs track and cross country. He is the reason I join. Although we don't like to admit it, younger brothers do idolize their older brothers. James and Lisa have graduated and moved on to college by now.

I am sure high school is a totally different experience for Matthew, especially on the social side. Matthew is one of the only whites at the school. Our high school is accepting of our family and Matthew is well liked. There are several black girls at school that find him attractive. Several times while walking down the halls a black girl grabs his butt. I would walk those same halls, over and over and even a few extra times and never once did I get a grab.

Matthew is very social and is able to function, as I am, in a black or white environment. He is at ease around blacks and that gains him credibility and respect among blacks.

The conversations among blacks about whites are the same. The "us against them" mentality still rings loudly. At times, it makes me uncomfortable because it can be too generalized and very unforgiving. Never do I speak out against it, but choose to disagree internally.

As I watch others interact with my white brother, I learn something that makes me proud to be black. Although Matthew is a minority, he is given access and is accepted among blacks. This happens over and over again. Although, the talk is unforgiving when it comes to whites, if a white person is able to function with ease around blacks that person is accepted. I deduce that because we, as blacks, have been the ones on the outside looking in, we are very tolerant and accepting when a white person makes the effort to be included. Matthew achieves this distinction and is often declared, "a cool white dude:" A very high title in our circle. This makes be proud of both Matthew and blacks that let him into their circle.

This is how I perceived Matthew's experience in high school, but I am sure his experience as one of the few whites in a black high school had many challenges. I am not so naïve to think he just skipped through his four years without any struggles. Again, I am certain he paid a higher cost in an environment where I was very comfortable.

Not all know how to deal with our family. The racial combination makes them a little nervous. This usually comes out in conversations where several blacks and I are sitting around talking. One person may say, "…then this white boy came up…" He stops mid-sentence. He looks up and then right at me and says, "Oh…no offense."

Again, I am not offended until he singles me out. It appears this same rule operates in the black community; the one that allows you to say something highly offensive as long as you say "No offense" at some point.

The racial balance that we as a family try to find is still not an easy one. High school grows into a place where I am able to exhale and be comfortable but the challenges are not completely erased.

In high school I not only learn more about myself but I learn more about how people see my friends and me. High School is a lot like grade school. The student body is black, the teachers are white and most of the schools we compete against are white.

Our high school has the reputation of being a very rowdy high school. The members of the football team and track team have the reputation everywhere of being cocky. They all wear black and white letterman's jackets that have their nick names stitched on the front and back. They have names like, "The Exterminator," "Bubba" "The Executioner" and "Dr. Doom".

Damon, a senior, adopts the nickname Damian the name of the devil in the very popular Omen movies. He has inscribed on the front of his jacket, "Damian" and underneath his nick name is tattooed "666" the sign of the devil. To do this at a Catholic high school is a little over the top.

Being a member of the track team, I get to know a lot of these guys and they are great guys; loud, boisterous, obnoxious guys, but decent guys. Their presentation of black makes me proud. Instead of blending into their surroundings, they are comfortable and confident in a skin that causes discomfort to so many. I adopt this lifestyle and become included with them.

Track becomes a large part of my high school experience and education. When the track team goes to invitational meets, which we do every Saturday from January to June, we are usually one of the only black schools present among a sea of schools. We give them "black" from the moment we step off the bus until the time we are taking home the first place trophy. Our presentation of "black" is anti-establishment. If it is acceptable to be quiet and calm, we give them loud and crazy. By presenting ourselves in this way we give the white schools that have very little contact with blacks a picture of "black" that is everything they expect.

Our sprinters dominate every event and we give them every stereotype there is and we are proud of it. Being teenagers we don't see how damaging that can be. The team is lightening fast, and we blast the latest rap music from our bus. Several members of the team spend more time talking to women than running. Their aggressive style is harmless but terrifying to some of the rural white girls we compete against.

We are heard before we are seen. Mr. Mack, the head track coach and athletic director, and Father Pat, the distance and cross country coach, struggle to keep the team out of trouble and focused. The superiority we feel is addictive. The power we possess fuels us. There is something intoxicating about dominating the white schools who we know don't like us. To be able to back up the talk, and in most cases be untouchable, is a nice feeling. In our minds, it is the polar opposite of society, so we cherish this feeling. Being super-human is a great feeling but it can be crushed in an instant.

The fall of my junior year, the Friday before homecoming, I arrive at school after Mom drops me off. Everybody is outside gathered around the field house. The night before, someone spray painted in large letters across the field house, "HOME OF THE SPEAR CHUCKERS." We are pretty confident that it has been done by some students from the white high school we will play in football the next day.

Mr. Mack tells us all to go to class and I don't think much about it the rest of the day. After school, I change into my practice gear to begin another cross country workout. The cross country team stretches out in the parking lot in front of the field house and this Friday is no different. We are stretching out and joking about the graffiti on the field house. Father Pat, our coach, hears us and shatters our calm stretching time as he yells, "THAT IS NOT FUNNY. THAT IS HOW THEY SEE YOU." The pain and frustration is all over his face. He tells us to finish stretching and go run. He does not tell us where or how far he just tells us to go run. Father Pat, the only white in the group, walks off disgusted.

As we are running to nowhere the gravity of the situation hits me. I understand what he is so upset about. It is the first time I comprehend the power of racism. To be viewed as something less than human and inferior, to be seen as savages hits me hard. Racism that I experience to this point is rarely so honest. I often wrestle with the thoughts that I am either being too sensitive or too paranoid. Racism rarely confirms the intention behind the action. It leaves me to fill in the blanks.

In big letters spray painted on _our_ field house is how the suburban school views us. We don't have to connect the dots; we don't have to search for the hidden answer. It is the most defining, real and devastating lesson I learn in high school.

Later in life, I learn just how much racism affected our lives at this point in my life.

13

BLACK LISTED

While we run through the neighborhood playing games and being kids, my parents work to provide us with our comfortable way of life. Mom is the director of the Myasthenia Gravis Foundation, an organization created to support those afflicted with this debilitating neuromuscular disease. Her office is on the sixth floor in the old part of Mount Carmel Hospital on Outer Drive and Schafer in Detroit. The best part of Mom's job is the annual fundraiser. Each year, Mom sends out hundreds of 3x5 parchment cards to mostly people in the entertainment field. The celebrities put on lipstick and kiss the 3x5 card leaving a kiss print. The card is autographed next to the kiss print and sent back to be auctioned off to raise money for Myasthenia Gravis.

It is exciting to see the kiss prints arrive. I remember kiss prints from Jack Lemon, Ann-Margret, Charles Schulz, Grace Slick, Phyllis Diller, Brooke Shields, Lucille Ball, Danny Thomas, Jackie Gleason, Christie Brinkely, Gilda Radner, Jean Stapleton, Vincent Price, Ahmad Rashad, Rita Moreno, and Carol Burnett. The kiss prints are then put on display at a local shopping mall for a few days and then auctioned off.

One year, Mom returns home from the auction with a special gift for me. It is a kiss print of Gary Coleman. Gary Coleman plays Arnold Jackson on the TV series "Different Strokes." He is the younger of the two black brothers who are adopted by Mr. Drummond, the wealthy white businessman. Arnold is the first famous adoptee I have ever seen. I am not sure Mom understands the powerful significance of this gift because I don't.

Dad remains the assistant to the Bishop for three years. After the three years, the Bishop's term has expired and he decides to accept a call to a church in Dayton, Ohio. The next Bishop is a very close friend of the head pastor at of the church in Dearborn, Dad's old boss. A career that had promise is brought to a halt with the placement of the new Bishop.

Dad has to start looking for a new church to pastor. In order to interview for a pastor's position, it is required that the potential pastor have the recommendation of the local Bishop. Before the present Bishop officially steps down he gives Dad the recommendations he needs to interview at some local churches. Hope has not totally disappeared but it has a timer attached to it that is ticking fast.

In the month's prior to the new Bishop taking office, the incoming Bishop confirms Dad's fear and lets the acting Bishop know, "There is no room in Michigan, for Pastor Hofmann." Dad will soon be shut out of all local Lutheran churches. The churches that are not local may grant Dad an interview but it will be without the help of his own Bishop. Many Churches will want to know what kind of pastor Dad is and they will logically go to his Bishop to find out. Dad's career was crashing in to the ceiling and the timer is ticking louder and louder.

Dad receives a call from a church in Warren Michigan, a city not too far from Detroit. The church is in a racially diverse neighbor and Dad thinks this will be a nice fit.

During the interview process Dad learns that the neighborhood surrounding the church is very diverse, but the church body is not. The existing members that go to the church have followed the white flight out of the city. The majority of the church members who used to live around the church have escaped to the white suburbs of Detroit.

On Sundays they make the trek back into Warren to have church because, unlike the members, the church building has not left. The church's lack of diversity and our family's abundant diversity is not a good match. After several interviews and Dad telling the church board of our unusual family, the church decides the parsonage that comes with the church will not be big enough for our family.

It is hard to believe there is a house smaller than the one we lived in on Whitcomb. They conclude that rather than inconvenience our family they will not offer Dad the job. It is far worse to live cramped than to be unemployed is their conclusion.

Dad gets another interview with a church in Indiana. He knows the local Bishop in Indiana and he gives Dad the required recommendation. The church is located in Valparaiso, Indiana. Naturally, it would mean the family would have to move, but Dad feels being a pastor is what he is called to do.

For the initial interview Dad is flown in to Indiana and he meets with the church board. At the interview, Dad feels compelled to tell them about our family. As Dad reveals that it would take more than one color from the Crayola box to draw our family portrait, the interview turns from an interview about pastoring a church to an interview about who I am going to date.

By this time, I am in high school and my choice of a girlfriend is a vital threat to the church and surrounding communities. Dad doesn't get a second interview and he doesn't want one after this conversation.

Dad knows the Bishop in charge of the Virginia territory and he calls him to find out if there is a church in need of a pastor. The Bishop follows procedure and recommends Dad for a position open in Richmond.

Once again, Dad boards a plane for an interview. Again, he feels honesty is the best way to handle our situation and he explains to the board in the interview the construction of our family. Surprisingly, the board doesn't flinch. There are no uncomfortable questions or concerns. The interview ends and Dad is excited. The interview went well with no hiccups.

Soon after returning home, Dad gets a call from the church in Richmond. They are very excited about Dad and invite him to return along with Mom. Mom and Dad are flown in to Richmond, Virginia. They are picked up from the airport and escorted by several members of the council to tour some local neighborhoods and potential houses. Mom and Dad decide that a local neighborhood that is more diverse will suit us the best. After a frustrating ordeal, it appears Dad has landed a job and a way to feed his family.

Mom and Dad stay several days in Richmond and through the weekend. They attend church where they sit and picture Dad in the pulpit giving his sermons. During church Dad is introduced to the church body and the excitement about a new pastor is evident. Immediately after church there is a coffee hour held to allow the church to meet their new pastor. As Mom sips her tea and socializes with the church members the subject of where they were going to live comes up. Mom explains that they like the diversity of a certain neighborhood and feel this neighborhood will be the best fit for our family. The church members surrounding Mom show their hand by the confused look on their faces. Mom realizes the make up of our family has not been explained to the church body. Feeling obligated, Mom explains our diverse family.

By now, Mom and Dad know the effects such an unusual family can have on a church so they make sure everyone was aware. Plus it was getting harder and harder to hide the little black kid on the end.

The council told Dad they would address this with the church body and now it is painfully evident the council failed to do so. Over tea, Mom explains the dynamics of our family. Nothing else is said about the conversation while Mom and Dad are visiting. Mom and Dad are taken to the airport later that afternoon and the council tells them to expect a call during the week to finalize everything.

The phone never rings.

Expecting the worse Dad finally calls and his expectations are realized. The church, whose leaders took them house-shopping less than a week ago, has changed their mind. They are no longer interested in Dad being their head pastor. The job that seems like a slam dunk, clangs off the rim loudly.

By now the new Bishop has taken over and the old bishop's recommendation has expired. All the favors Dad has with other Bishops have run out too. The ability to provide for his family is becoming narrower.

While Dad continues to look for a church, he finds a job as an interim pastor at a church in Lima, Ohio, about two hours south of Detroit. Dad packs up on Tuesday of each week and leaves early Wednesday to go to Lima, Ohio to serve as a pastor, while the church looks for a full time pastor. I get up for my paper route early Wednesday and on my dresser each week is a note from Dad. In his distinctive, deceivingly neat but near illegible writing, Dad jots a short note to each of us kids. He tells us to have a good week and he will see us on Sunday afternoon. Dad travels I-75 to and from Lima for about three months, to stay busy and to get exposure hoping this will lead to another church in need of a pastor. The lead never comes and the need to get permanent employment is more pressing.

A position at a local hospital, as the Director of the Employee Assistance Program, comes available. Dad had gone to University of Detroit and earned a Masters Degree in counseling many years before which qualified him for the hospital job. For the first time in a long time he goes to an interview and the racial make up of his family does not dominate the interview. In fact, it never comes up. Dad is hired quickly. It is not Dad's dream job but it is a small sacrifice to maintain our family's way of life.

After about six years, due to hospital cut backs, they slash Dad's salary by $10,000. I hear Mom and Dad talking about it and how hard it was going to be for us and I get that same sick feeling in my stomach I had the weeks that followed the purse snatching incident.

Dad endures the job at the hospital until 2 years later they cut the job completely. Dad decides to sell Life Insurance instead of going through more disappointing interviews with closed minded churches.

I am never privy to any of this while it happens. Mom and Dad never share the stories of the disappointing interviews while they are happening. While in high school I was never aware that we almost moved to Richmond, Virginia.

I am aware of the changes in jobs but just assume every now and then adults change jobs. The only job change that affects me is when we move to Shaftsbury and that is a great and needed change. All the other changes and the dynamics behind I find out about as I interview Mom and Dad for this book.

Mom and Dad did a great job of shielding me from all of the ugliness that they faced. I walk through a lot of it not even noticing what is going on around me. I walk through it all not realizing the stress Mom and Dad are feeling. It isn't until I am in my late twenties that it occurs to me that parents have bad days, they get sick, and they bleed if they get cut. As I sit down to write this book and begin talking to Mom and Dad about our unique situation, the stories that went on around me come out. There are more stories of adversity that come out in between my games of Baseball and Ditch It.

Dad tells a story about us going camping when I was about three years old. He and I walk up to the office to rent a site to camp. The owner looks at Dad and he looks at he and me refuses to rent us a spot. He says they are all filled but looking at the campground, it is obvious there are several spots available. We turn and walk away and Dad realizes there isn't much he could do. We get back in the car and drive to the next campground where we are welcomed without any questions.

Mom tells me the story of us going to see some old friends from Dearborn, a fellow pastor and his family. We are camping near their new home in Wisconsin and put them on our itinerary. Our friends have family visiting from out of town when we are in town. Their extended family is not as open minded as our friends so in order to visit means they have to come see us at the campground. I would not be welcomed by the extended family.

It is every parent's desire to shield his or her children from the ugliness of the world. Mom and Dad are handed shovel after shovel of ugly and I never know about it. The sacrifices they make for me are never realized until the ordeals are small memories in the rearview mirror. These reoccurring stories of prejudice whether blatant or subtle occur around me, but not to me. Mom and Dad spread their parental wings over me and protect me from the ugly. Knowing all of this was a direct result of my presence would have crippled me when they occurred. Instead it falls on their shoulders and I continue my games of Baseball and Ditch it without knowing the pain and struggle they endure.

Hearing story after story of how unjustly our family was treated again humbles me. In my head I wonder if their extreme decision to adopt me was too costly. At every turn it seems the family is affected by my presence. I am grateful but I am not sure if I am worth the high price they paid. My parents will say it is all worth it but this is something I must ponder. Their protection of me from all this is far beyond amazing.

Unfortunately, the microscopic particles of hate occasionally seep through, and I return the favor by shielding Mom and Dad.

14

MY FIRST

Vocabulary Lesson 1

Black:
A crayon or a stick of licorice

Oreo:
One small black round cookie
Sweet white filling
One small back round cookie

Coon:
A fury black masked animal

Spear Chucker:
A primitive hunter

Jungle Bunny
An exotic rabbit

Spook:
A tiny ghost like creature

Porch Monkey
A small primate who inhabits a porch

Every year my family and I go on vacation. It is usually for a week or two in the summer. All six of us and Trixie, the family collie, pile into our car. The pop up camper is attached to the car, and we drive to our destination.

My mother is the ultimate planner and every minute is accounted for. On day one, we drive six hours and stop off at the KOA campground five miles off the freeway. We set up camp, and enjoy the campground for two and half days and then pack up and head to the next destination. This is the type of itinerary we follow. Included in the itinerary are stops to the local town to get food and stock up. There is one trip to the local grocery store when I was eight years old I will never forget.

The six of us arrive at the grocery store. Trixie stays back at the campground attached to the camper by her leash. In the car on the way, we are given the traditional "pre-shopping" schedule. We are told there is a shopping list and we will not deviate from it. No extras, no add-ons, no treats. The car rolls into the parking lot and the mission is about to begin. As soon as Dad puts the car in park we all spill out. Mom is the commander and chief and she is focused on getting everything on the list cheaper than anyone else has in the history of mankind. To say money is tight for a family of six, on a Lutheran Minister's salary, is the biggest understatement in the history of mankind.

To Mom's credit no one has every stretched a dollar like she does. Somehow the elastic in our dollars are stretched further than the elastic on Dad's Fruit of the Looms. We descend upon the grocery store like a Green Beret unit. Mom is in charge of getting us out alive with the budget still breathing. As mission commander, Mom has no respect for the honor code, "No one gets left behind." There are many incidents where she would turn a corner and disappear into the produce section leaving us kids to wonder where she went. Sometimes, she fakes one way, sees a sale on canned goods and goes another and leaves the four kids dumbfounded. If you aren't careful someone is leaving the store with a fractured ankle. Her moves can snap an ankle like a twig.

Dad is never stressed. He is like an old war dog. He is very familiar with the drill and able to track Mom through the store. Often times he is gone for several minutes but picks up Mom's scent in baked goods and falls right back in line. It probably isn't too hard to find a family with four children who loath the food reconnaissance missions like we do. We have no reservations about voicing our displeasure.

On this particular mission, we walk around the grocery store for what feels like hours. As we shop, we keep crossing the path of a white family who has a boy about my age, seven or eight. I manage to keep one eye on Mom and one eye on him. We see each other at the end of an aisle or a few aisles over and we make eye contact. We start making faces at each other and this game goes on for the majority of our marathon bargain hunt. I see him and I stick out my tongue and then he sees me and pushes his nose up to make a pig nose, or I give him the thumbs up and he returns my gesture with the thumbs down signal. This is a great way to distract me from the grueling task of comparing prices.

Finally, we complete our mission. We have gotten the best price on corn, hamburger and hot dogs, baked beans, paper plates, plastic forks and aluminum foil. There is no way we could have gotten a better deal unless we stole the corn and a pig from a nearby farm and ate it with our bare hands.

Quickly, we pay and it is time to rendezvous back at the Hofmann vehicle. This is when the traditional dance begins between my parents and us kids. This store has the gumball machines and candy machines in the front entrance area of the store and just outside the store are small penny rides. There is a horse, and a car calling my name as they sit idle.

I know the rules; I can't make an audible request for money. If I want candy, or gum, or a ride, I realize the price of that will have to be multiplied by four and there is no way we are going to ruin the vacation by blowing the money we just saved on such luxuries as candy, gum, or a horse that slowly moves up and down for one minute. But the kid in me has to at least try. I slow down and look longingly at the beautiful multi-colored gum and candy. Then I look back at Mom and then Dad. My face lights up with a smile at the possibility of getting a coveted piece of gum. It has never worked up to this point but the hope sends adrenaline through my body. Maybe today my cunning plan will work. My parents know the routine and they pretend not see me. I try to slow the caravan but there is no use, they keep on walking past the gum ball machines. This time I have an idea, I will run up ahead to the rides, this way I will have more time to really give them an Oscar winning performance. There should be no way I will be denied.

As I ran up ahead I notice my friend from the store is riding the horse. Here is my chance, my acting ability combined with another kid whose parents obviously love him enough to let him ride. I know I am golden.

As I am waiting for just the right time to give my parents my look, I stroll by the boy on the plastic hollow steed. He is selling the ride. He has on jeans, cowboy boots, and a t-shirt and is riding the horse like it is a wild mustang. This is my first chance to see him up close. I want to impress him so I go for the sure thing. I am a big fan of the TV show, *Happy Days,* and think The Fonz is the coolest man on the planet. I stroll by my friend and give him my best Arthur Fonzerelli impression complete with both thumbs up and a "Heeeeeeey". He looks down at me with a half smile that seems more evil and sinister than friendly.

"Nigger!" He says softly.

He knows my parents are too far behind to hear him and his parents are nowhere in site. Suddenly the importance of riding the horse vanishes and I am changed. Time is paused. This boy who I thought was my friend is really the opposite. In an instant I realize the playing that we were doing in the store was not friendly on his part. He was antagonizing me. I just never got close enough to him in the store to realize it.

The utterance of that word steals life from me. I go from being a 7-year-old kid on vacation, to small and black in an environment that has very few people like me. That word takes me immediately to a place where I am alone and different.

Until then I hadn't noticed that in this small rural town I haven't seen one other black person the whole time we are there. I feel like I have lost with no way to win at this playful-turned-evil game we play. This mature realization floods my mind all in a matter of one step. I am certain in that one step my whole demeanor changes and part of my childhood innocence is assassinated in the same instant. Defeated I walk away and never mentioning to my parents what happened. I shield them from the ugliness.

I still picture the expression on his face. He is proud and convinced he is superior. He is so convincing that *I* believe it. In this instant, I learn that this word is a very powerful word; A word that has no rebuttal. There is no other word in the English language that can conjure up so much emotion. It is a word that always frustrates me. When a white person says that to you no matter what you say back there is no word as demeaning, degrading and devaluing as Nigger.

I do not consider myself a violent person but I know if a white person were to call me a Nigger today I feel justified to respond with a possessed rage that would make the Tyson/Holyfield ear biting incident look rational and understandable.

In the late 60's early 70's nigger is used more frequently. Today the word has been changed from nigger to the "N" word. It is understood that it is not a word to be used openly. Even typing the whole word makes me uncomfortable.

Growing up it is a weapon. Soon after my first nigger I begin to hear it more and more. It is like the whole world discovered nigger the same day I did. I realize my sensitivity is heightened to the word, which makes me more aware of it.

My brothers begin to use it. It becomes their first weapon of choice when we are arguing and I have no response. My best response is to pretend it doesn't affect me. My Mom, Dad, and Lisa never use the word and I am never concerned that that is a possibility with them.

My brothers use it for its affect rather than the meaning. As pre-teenagers, they have no idea of the gravity of the word. In the heat of battle you use the most lethal weapon. You don't stop to analyze the social and moral aspects of using it. You use it to incapacitate your enemy and this is what they did.

I mention this to some of my friends who are black and they are appalled. I don't put that much weight in it when it comes from my brothers. Do I really think they mean it? No, they are attacking my weak point and doing what they can to win a fight. As we get older, they grow to understand the word and use it less and less.

In high school, I find out we are like most families. There are certain things you can say about family but no one outside the family gets that same privilege. That is how it is with us. An incident occurs in high school that I will never let vanish from my memory.

The incident occurs during my junior year. It involved Matthew, who was a senior at the time and had a profound affect on me.

Even though we had our differences growing up, Matthew is my best friend, especially in our early years. Because we were so close in age we were each other's playmate. I also think because we are such an unusual family there was comfort in each other. When I was the minority, because of his experiences, he understood what I was going through. When he was the minority, I understood too. Matthew and I extend this friendship as we became teammates on the track and cross country teams in high school.

My junior year, I injure my leg and spend the majority of track season rehabbing from my injury.

Initially, even though I am injured, I go to the meets and cheer my team on. After awhile, it is too depressing to go. To sit and watch people win races that I knew I could if I was healthy is more painful than my injury. I choose to stay home and work at rehabbing my leg instead of watching this torture.

One Thursday, as I headed home, the track team assembles, absent me and competes against another local Catholic high school. Our high school has become a powerhouse in track and this meet should be very uneventful. Again, the competition is the same; our mostly black school against a mostly white school. Although the competition on the track will not be much, the meeting of an all black school and an all white school in Detroit often made the uneventful eventful.

The team we faced on that Thursday had one runner I knew very well, Eugene Crampfish. He had become my number one rivalry and was the only one to beat me at the state cross country meet the fall before. He was a wiry white kid who was about 5'6" and 130 pounds and had a mouth that moved several seconds before his brain.

At this particular track meet, something happened between Eugene and my brother Matthew. My friend, Derrick Louis, called me later that night and gave me a play by play of the incident.

Derrick didn't know how it started but all of a sudden across the track he could hear Matthew screaming at Eugene. Everyone ran towards the shouting hoping to see a fight. Matthew and Eugene were yelling back and forth and as Derrick got closer he could hear they were arguing about ME, and Matthew is defending ME!

Then Eugene said something under his breath that only Matthew could hear and Matthew lost it. All rational thought and behavior left Matthew. He charged at Eugene and from everyone's account, it was obvious Matthew was going to kill Eugene right on the infield of the track. Several coaches, including Father Pat our distance coach, jumped in between them, more for Eugene's safety than anything else. Normally, once our coach, Father Pat, got involved that was the end of it. That Thursday it didn't matter. Matthew could not see or hear Father Pat through the red he saw and the alarms going off in his head.

Matthew kept charging after Eugene pushing past Father Pat. Some of our teammates tried to pull Matthew away and calm him down but it didn't work. Matthew was determined to separate Eugene's head from his body.

Eugene was conflicted. There was a strange chemical reaction going on in Eugene's body. His testosterone was telling him to stay there and fight, but his adrenaline was screaming," RUN, EUGENE, RUN." He didn't know which signal was more rational. Matthew's storm of fury confused Eugene. Eugene didn't count on this volcanic reaction. Instead, Eugene sat there and didn't say or do much. The chemical reaction froze his brain and he stood there in a catatonic state. Eugene wasn't sure what this crazy white boy was going to do to him and his posture showed Eugene didn't want to find out. He made sure there were plenty of people between him and Matthew.

Eventually, Mr. Mack, our head track coach and school disciplinarian stepped in to save Eugene's life. Mr. Mack is feared by EVERYBODY. He is a stocky 5'8" white man with horned rimmed glasses and a brush cut and no one has ever stood up to him. His loud bark would immediately cause what ever was in your bladder to sprint out.

When he steps in, the confrontation is defused and rational thought immediately returned to Matthew. Matthew was sent to the team bus and not allowed to compete that day.

My imagination has convinced me Eugene called me a nigger. After all, one white guy calling a black guy a nigger in front of another white guy, who's gonna say anything? Who's it gonna hurt?

Eugene had made a similar mistake during a basketball game the season before. Eugene called one of our players a nigger during a game and Eugene's nose had been crooked ever since. His mouth still was way ahead of his brain. He probably assumed on the track that the lonely white guy on our team would not object to the "N" word. Eugene didn't figure the lonely white guy was my brother.

What Matthew did that day was very risky. He risked being tagged as the "crazy white boy." Interestingly enough, that moment of mindless rage earned Matthew a lot of respect from the blacks at school. They all saw it as Matthew just trying to neutralize an enemy that deserved to be neutralized.

In the end, it doesn't matter to me what was said or how it looked. All I know is my big brother stood up for me. Matthew never said anything about the track meet when he got home and after talking to Derrick that night, I never asked Matthew about it.

We still fought after this but the word takes another hiatus; only to return one last time a few years later.

We were both home from college on spring break at the end of my first year of college. Matthew had brought his girlfriend with him. We had gotten into it again (over what I don't know specifically). Matthew was trying to still prove he was the big brother. We are yelling back and forth and I was not backing down as I usually did. My first year at college was a racial awakening and I was sick and tired of being treated like a second class citizen at college and refused to be treated like it at home. Matthew was frustrated with the fact that the fight was not going as easy as usual and resorted to calling in an air strike. Matthew began to shout at me, in front of his girlfriend "you ni…". He never got the full word out.

I lunged at Matthew and pushed him into the Grandfather Clock made by our Grandfather for my mother that sat in the corner of the foyer. I was prepared to put him through it if I had to. To my surprise Matthew didn't fight back. This was shocking because growing up Matthew was a fighter, a scrapper. This time, he backed off and looked at me like all rational thought and behavior had left me.

The grandfather clock clanged and shook from side to side. This violent noise brought Dad out of his upstairs office. Dad stormed down the steps in what seems like one quick motion and ended up between Matthew and me.

Dad rarely got involved in disciplining us as that was part of Commander Mom's responsibilities, so whenever he did get involved we knew it was in our best interest to quit doing whatever it was we were doing.

"What is going on? What is this about?" Dad demanded.

Matthew and I both responded in unison, "Nothing."

The fight ended there in front of the swinging, bonging Grandfather clock. Once again I didn't feel Dad needed to hear about this ugly word that had crept into our house over and over again.

The relationship Matthew and I had changed that day and at that moment. The verbal and physical battles stopped. We came to a place of mutual respect and admiration that we couldn't get to without something like that happening. The word was buried and Matthew finally understood from my reaction, the gravity of that word.

The utterance of this one word was not as damaging as the silence I allowed around it. Growing up I thought if I ignored how this word made me feel, I could eliminate its affect on me. My poor attempt to combat hate and violence with silence failed. Instead I gave much more power to this word and the incidents attached to it.

I am often asked if I would have changed anything regarding the way I was raised and for many years I would quickly say no.

As I put my thoughts to this page I have a first and last regret. I regret that we didn't talk much about race or its affects on us in our home. We were destined to be affected by it and ignoring it only gave it power it didn't deserve. Since we didn't openly talk about race, I would go on to make decisions without the knowledge of how race could affect those decisions.

15

DECISIONS

The starter's pistol shatters the silent November air. The 100 of us who qualify for the State cross country meet take off. This is my senior year and my last high school cross country race. The ground of the golf course shakes as we head towards the first turn. 200 yards in to the race I look around and find that I am tied for last place. I look to my right and there is Mike. We are numbers 99 and 100.

The rest of the runners are ahead of us but instinctively we don't panic. We look at each other and then around us and I say, "Okay, lets go get 'em, one at a time." We pick up our pace but realize this is a three mile race; no need to sprint at this point. Slowly one by one we move up. We stay side by side for the first mile passing one over-excited runner after another. Mike is a sophomore so to be at the state meet is an honor. There are very few sophomores running this course today.

We both continue to move up but now at a different pace. We lose each other in the large crowd and my eyes are concentrated on the back of the head of the runner in front of me. I tell myself over and over again, "One at a time. One at a time."

It is a trick I have learned. I try to concentrate on anything but what my body feels. I try to trick my body into to just moving forward. I ignore the lungs that are screaming, "Slow down we need more air."

I am coming off a bad injury from last spring and wasn't expected to qualify for the state meet. Father Pat, my coach, for the first time, doesn't tell me where he expects me to finish. He knows I have lost a lot of valuable training time trying to heal. My cardiovascular fitness is not where it needs to be to compete in a race like this. Father Pat just tells me to run well.

I am in the race now and my competiveness wants to prove to Father Pat that I can do well. Father Pat mentions to me just before the race that if I finish in the top 10 he will be surprised. I have no idea what to expect or where I should finish. I only know each person I pass gets me closer to the finish line.

Since I started out the race being so far behind, I have no idea how far ahead the leaders are in the race. The only thing I can do is, "one at a time."

Once I pass that one, I look ahead to the next head I must focus in on. I look *ahead* 50 yards to the next head. I train my eyes to concentrate on his hair. I focus on how his hair moves with each step. I hear and see nothing else but his hair flopping up and down. I also concentrate on my breathing. I breathe in rhythm with my strides and this takes my mind off the lack of oxygen.

I am one of the only blacks in the race and that motivates me to do better. To do well in a sport that is dominated by whites gives me a passion to do better than I am expected to do. The "us" versus "them" mentality in a strange way motivates me to prove I am just as good as the white runners.

One by one I continue to move up. As I pass each runner, I look for any signs of weakness in them. I look for heavy breathing or an awkward stride. This shows me they are tired. I refuse to give them any signs of the same, so I improve my stride making it smooth and silent. My feet touch the grass without sound. As I pass them I hold my breath. This has to look effortless and easy. I pick up the pace for the next 20-25 yards. I do not want them to go with me, so I have to pass them quickly.

I continue up and down the rolling hills of the golf course. Some hills are as steep as 45 degrees and I use them to crush the spirit of any runner around me. Sprinting up a hill, I pass a few more who are struggling to make it to the top. At the top of the hill out of ear shot I gasp for air and recover.

Constantly and methodically, I move through the course until I can see what looks like heaven, the finish line.

The finish line is now 400 yards away. This gives me energy and I see three or four people within striking distance. I set out for the first one. As I pass him, he tries to go with me. I know I have to beat him now to make sure he doesn't come back closer to the finish. I usually wait for the last 100 yards to begin my sprint but I can't afford to have this runner hang with me. He picks up his pace and I pick up mine. He is still there and I have to shake him, NOW!

The sooner I leave him, the sooner I can slow down to recover before my last sprint to the finish.

He will not back off and now it is a battle of who will give in first. I increase my pace and so does he. We are stride for stride and I am running out of room. This game has taken up 100 yards and I have got to dispose of him now. I decided if he is going to beat me I will drain him of all his energy to do so. I begin to sprint, breathing in and out, still in rhythm, as if I am in labor. My lungs are about to explode, but I have to finish him now. I swing my arms back further and lengthen my stride. He drops back one step and then two and I feel him surrender. The fracturing of his will makes a distinct noise. I have broken him.

He will not come back but my energy is depleted. The two or three runners that I had a chance at I can't get. I am running on fumes. The next 100 yards I use to recover. I expand my chest to take in as much air as possible; I need to fill my lungs. As I do, I listen. The fear of footsteps behind me is distracting. I listen and I hear nothing. To turn around and look is a sign of fear and weakness and if someone is in striking distance they will consume me if they see me turn around. I watch the fans that have lined the last 100 yards to the finish and their eyes are on me and not behind me which tells me there is no one close to me.

It is time to go again; up on my toes and go; time to leave every ounce of energy on this cold golf course. I begin to pick up the pace and within 20 yards I am at a full sprint. The finish line races toward me and I lean in across it. Now I can feed my lungs the air they have been craving.

Father Pat meets me just beyond the finish line and I just want to hear the number ten. He is excited and asks, "Do you know what place you got." I am still panting and feeding my lungs. I squeeze out "No." He grabs me and hugs me and picks me off my feet. "You got fifth!" The energy I lost over the last three miles comes flooding back to me. The top seven get the distinction of All-State honors. I passed 95 people and I am All-State for the second year.

I got it right.

My performance gets me noticed by colleges and I begin getting letters and phone calls from some colleges and universities. One day while sitting around the house the phone rings. There is a loud and excited man on the other end. He asks for me and he explains he is from a small private college up north. I have never heard of the college before but I don't tell him that information. He introduces himself, as Coach Charles Gray, the cross country and distance coach for the college. He tells me to keep up the good work and congratulates me on my success. I hang up the phone and am excited some college would call to talk to me.

Over the next few months I don't hear much from anyone. I get information in the mail from several colleges and really don't give anyone much thought. I enjoy my high school experience and am not looking forward to leaving. Over the past four years I have gotten very comfortable with myself and my place in high school. I am not part of the popular crowd, but I am not part of the crowd everyone ignores either.

My athletic ability has grabbed attention and made me moderately popular. Running track has saved my life socially. My success in track has given me confidence and the opportunity to allow people to get to know me. Because my high school is such a small school, the confidence I gain in track gives me the courage to be more social. I am a long way from the closed off freshman I was four years ago.

Winter indoor track begins and we flow quickly into regular track. I have trained hard over the off-season and I am ready to end my high school track career with success. As we begin track the rumors of our track team being state champs starts right away. The year before while I was injured and sitting at home, our track team went to the state meet and returned home state champs. I pray I can complete this track season injury free.

I do well throughout the season being moderately successful along the way. As we enter April we begin to prepare for the important meets. One day while practicing, I notice a pain in my right foot. I ignore it hoping it will go away. It doesn't and stays with me for two weeks. The nagging pain forces to mention it to my coach. This is only after he notices me limping.

Father Pat acts immediately. He calls a friend who is a doctor and we drive 30 minutes to nowhere and the doctor examines my foot and takes x-rays all free of charge. Father Pat uses the priest thing to his advantage and does a great job of talking people into anything. In minutes the doctor is back to show us an invisible crack in one of the bones of my foot. I have a stress fracture and although I can't see it on the x-ray, I can see the rest of my season quickly fading away.

Resigned, I am ready to leave, but Father Pat is not ready to give up so quickly. He asks the doctor what we can do. The doctor states he has a friend that could design a shoe to protect my foot.

We go see the friend who is also a foot doctor and he confiscates my shoes. We return a few days later. He has installed in the soles of my shoes steel rods to adsorb the impact and protect my feet. He has to put them in both shoes because they add a noticeable amount of weight to the shoe and running with only one weighted shoe would throw off my stride. We take my new heavy shoes and we leave. The redesigning of my shoe could not have been cheap, but I never see a bill. Father Pat works his priestly magic again or he pays for it and doesn't tell me.

I practice with the shoes and soon the pain is gone and I am back on schedule.

We arrive at the regional meet; I finish both the mile and two mile in first place and qualify for the state meet.

Coach Grey, from the small private college calls later that same night.

"Hi coach, yes I ran well today. I qualified for the state meet in the mile and two mile races." I held the phone away from my ear as coach Gray lets out an excited cackle.

"What place did you get?" he asked. "I finished first in both I proudly state." Habit causes me to back away from the phone again. When he calms down he tells me he will be at the state meet to watch me run. He wishes me good luck and ends the conversation.

I wait two weeks for the state meet to get here and I am nervous and excited. I love to compete in these races. The distance races are always dominated by tall skinny white kids. When I was just starting to run well my junior year, I loved to look down the starting line and see that I was the shortest and the darkest of all the runners. I am sure they never counted me as their competition.

Our school is known for their sprinters. We were always thought to be one of the best track teams in the state because of our sprinters and relay teams.

The state meet is my chance to show in the white dominated events that blacks can compete with them too. The racial pride that I adopted in grade school has grown to inspire and motivate me.

The team arrives in Jackson, Michigan the night before to prepare for the meet. We get our room assignments and then the sprinters, the shot-putter, and I meet out by the pool. It is not the pool that attracts us but the girls' track team from Benton Harbor who has congregated there. Some couple up and disappear, but most stay and just talk. I meet a sprinter and she is surprised to know I run distance. She is even more surprised when my coach comes down with the program of tomorrow's meet. It has the times of each runner from their regional races. As we expect our sprinters and relays have run the fastest or second fastest in most events. My mile and two mile times are the fastest for both races. I am the one to beat in both of my events. Coach could not have come at a more perfect time. I can see in this young lady's face she is impressed.

Coach announces loudly that we have to go get dinner. He pulls us away from our new friends. Father Pat, believes girls make you run slower, so he does what he can to break us all apart. We return to our rooms to get ready for dinner and to break up one couple that found their way to one of the beds. This sprinter wasn't only fast on his feet.

We go to dinner and my excited stomach won't allow me to eat much. We discuss our chances at being repeat champions and our chances are good. A high school from Flint, who seems to always have a strong team is still strong and it appears we will compete with them for the championship. Flint is also strong in the sprints. They do not have any distance runners with them. Father Pat comments that I may be the difference between first and second place tomorrow. The pressure inspires me.

We return to our hotel rooms and Father Pat is in for a long night. He stations himself in the hall outside our hotel rooms. He stands guard so no one can leave or come in, mainly the girls' track team be met before.

We call back and forth to the girl's rooms and we devise a plan. We tell them to come over but come around to the back of the room; the balcony side. Father Pat stations us on the second floor making it more difficult to escape. The girls are standing below our balcony and we let down a bed sheet. One by one our shot-putter pulls them up.

We sit and joke for hours with the girls and then we lower them down and they go back to their room. One of our sprinters wants to go back with them so we lower him down too. We all go to bed at about 3:00 am. Then the phone rings. Our sprinter is caught in the girls' room. Their coach is now walking the hallway to make sure they don't escape. For the next hour he calls to our room over and over again. He finally escapes and makes it back to our room. At about 4:00 am we get to sleep.

At 7:30 Father Pat pounds on our door and tells us to be ready in 30 minutes to go to breakfast. We meet at the van at 8:00 am.

Shortly after breakfast, we arrive at the track that is decked out ready to host a state meet. We all scatter to prepare for our races and events. I have plenty of time, so I go and find the friend I met last night and we walk around most of the day. My mind is not on the races.

I have a routine to prepare for my races. I usually go to bed about 10:00 pm the night before, visualize each lap of each race, memorize my split times for each lap, pray and go to bed. At the meet, before each of my races I would go over each race again. I would stretch out, warm up and be ready to race. Today was much different. I was functioning on very little sleep and I was too distracted by this cute sprinter to go through the races.

As I am walking around and doing some stretching, I see several college coaches who know me. There are the coaches from Eastern Michigan University, Western Michigan University, Sienna Heights College, and Spring Arbor College. They all wish me luck. Coach Gray runs up to me and hugs me and is much more excited in person. He wishes me luck and tells me he will talk to me later.

I am too busy laughing and flirting with my sprinter friend to notice my race is about to start. Father Pat hunts me down and yells for me to report in on the track. I do so and we start the mile race.

The race starts fast and again I know not to panic. I then try to shift in to second gear and nothing happens. I try to concentrate on the head in front of me but I can't focus. I try to pick up the pace but as I do those in front of me do too. Then they do the unexpected. They start to pull away from me and I can do nothing to hold on. The race finishes well before I do. I end up in eighth place. I do secure a medal and two points for the team. My brain is fried and I don't know why.

I return to the stands and talk things over with Father Pat. We agree the mile is over and I must prepare for the two mile.

The two mile, which is usually the race I do better in, goes even worse than the mile. My energy and focus is gone and I do good just to finish. I do not finish in the top eight so I get no medal and no points for the team.

I return to the stands and Father Pat consoles me. I feel terrible and all the coaches who spoke to me earlier just look at me and don't say a word. I retreat down the steps to go get my sweats and I meet up with my sprinter friend. She consoles me by giving me an unexpected hug.

We walk around the track and a sprinter from River Rouge High School runs up to me and points at me. "Man I lost some duckets on you. What happened?" I just walk away. There were other black schools like River Rouge who I have seen all year and they also enjoy watching a short black kid beat the tall white kids.

The sprinters have done well all day. They keep us in the hunt for the championship. After my race Father Pat totals up our score and although the meet isn't over we determine it is impossible for us to win. We take second. We lose to the high school from Flint by eight points. I was expected to bring in 20 points and I brought in 2. Father Pat was right. The championship would come down to me. It would take me years to get over this failure.

My close friends, Derrick Louis, Greg James and Steve Butler, drove up to watch me run and I decide to ride back home with them. The ride back in the van would not be a pleasant one with the sprinters. As I am leaving Coach Gray stops me. "Well, today just wasn't your day. We would still love to see ya running for us." We shake hands and he says he will call me.

Later that summer, my parents drop me off at the small private college to begin my college career. My decision is based on the fact that Coach Gray never gave up on me. I ignore the fact that the student body at the college is 99% white. I never discuss or consider how I will fit in, in an environment that is all white all the time.

16

OPPRESSION

The door to my small dorm room closes and the sound bounces off the empty walls. Mom and Dad just hugged me and said goodbye and I sit on my small bed alone. My new bed is about 150 miles north of Detroit at a private Presbyterian College. I am trying to rationalize in my head why I chose to come here. The academic answer is to study Exercise Physiology so I can become a physical therapist, but my question is far beyond the academic answer. This college is the whitest place I have ever seen. The student body is about 1100 students and of those 1100 I will soon find out 13 are black and mostly from the Detroit area. What did I agree too?

As I walk across campus and take classes I realize how unique Detroit is. Although I live in a neighborhood that is predominately white, everywhere I go in Detroit I see black people. Detroit is my protected bubble. I don't have to go far to be part of a majority. My white in Detroit was really tan. This college white is blinding. Detroit has shielded me from living as a true minority.

College is a more realistic view of America. I now live among people who do not understand what being black is like. I am shocked to learn at a freshmen gathering that there are some in my new community who have never seen a black person in real life. The closest some have come to a black person is watching them on TV. In 1985 there are still very few positive portrayals of blacks on TV.

I resent that and a confusing anger boils in me. I realize that for some exposure to another race is optional. For minorities it is unavoidable. The fact that some can carry out their lives without ever having to come in contact with any other cultures causes my anger to always be just below boiling temperatures. The luxury of having this choice (a choice I have never and will never have) makes me mad.

As lopsided as Detroit is racially, I could never go a day without seeing a white person. The knowledge that there are some cities where there are no blacks and that those cities can get along without blacks hits me hard. They have no need for people like me and I feel that as I walk to class.

I feel powerless because my section of this new population has no voice. What I find even more infuriating is that those of us who have this common bond can't get along. I find there are some blacks who do not wish to associate with other blacks. I guess they think if they are seen with us, people will realize they too are black. I quickly write them off as "sell outs" and kick them out of my community. Surprisingly, they don't need us and they function fine without us.

My first week of my freshman year, as I am walking out of my dorm, I see a dark skinned black student. He sees me and right away comes up to me and starts a conversation. I am starved for the human contact that I am used to. We strike a bond right away. He is from Brooklyn, New York. He is Jamaican so his Brooklyn/Jamaican accent right away makes him interesting. His name is Lindley and sophomore year we become roommates. We both joke about how we landed in the middle of white America coming from two of the blackest cities in America. We keep each other afloat as we tread through these foreign waters. We virtually cut off all the other blacks because of their lack of blackness. Their lack of blackness is defined as their desire to associate more with the white population than the black population. I am not sure if we cut them off first or vice versa.

The other blacks are more mainstream and put on the disguise of being white and Lindley and I have no desire to do so.

Our dorm room is our fortress of solitude. We stay up until all times of the night laughing about how crazy this white place is to us. Because we feel like a contagious disease, we don our blackness to the highest degree. We give them every stereotype they expect. We are loud, rude and mean. We sport do rags, Africa medallions and often times our speech is incomprehensible to those around us. Our slang is as thick as we can make it. It is our way of keeping them at a distance.

Needless to say we don't fit in very well and our egos tell us it's ok.

This is the first time in my life I feel what oppression is like. This system is so unfairly weighted that I have no chance at winning. To speak up and complain is seen as weak and I will be labeled too sensitive. Instead, I learn to say nothing.

I clearly remember, one evening, I was in my dorm room lying on my bed studying. A group of my cross country teammates had been drinking and they passed by my room. My door is slightly open and as my teammates walk by they see me and spill into my room. A white student who makes the mistake of thinking we are closer than we actually are jumps on top of me and pins me down. His freckled face is inches from mine as he sits on my chest and I can't move. He puts his finger on my nose and loudly states, "You're black!" He laughs loudly and the others with him do not know what to do. I hear silence broken with nervous laughter and slowly they all pour out of my room. I am left feeling helpless and ashamed. Ashamed that I did not decapitate him right there. That feeling that I have grown to know so well growing up quickly comes back. Now everyone knows it. I am different again.

For the next few weeks at cross country practice I am very cold towards my freckled faced teammate. He notices something is wrong and confronts *me* about *my* attitude. He clearly remembers the incident and our versions of the story are identical. He can't understand why I am so upset. My feelings are dismissed and his conscience writes it off as me being too sensitive. This new life is a crazy mirror image of life I am used to and what I see as clearly wrong is somehow justified as right.

It is this tilted justice and my awareness of it day after day that wears on me. It is not as obvious as someone shouting nigger at me everyday but the effects are the same. It is how I am treated differently on a daily basis that crushes my self-esteem. When a white person who I am friendly with greets his white friends with "hi," and greets me with, "what's up," I feel that difference like a coat that is too small wrapped around me. When a white friend shakes the hand of another white friend and offers me a high five or grabs my hand and wrestles with it in his attempt to give his version of a black hand shake, I am again shoved in the box set apart from everyone else.

When I come around the corner in my dorm and I hear someone giving their imitation of what a black person sounds like and he immediately stops when he sees me, I feel like an outcast. It is the thought that every conversation I have with a white student could involve some unconscious or conscious slip of the tongue that directs all the attention to me, and that makes we want to pull away. I resolve that if I'm going to be seen as different, it will be on my terms, not theirs.

I realize even twenty years after my four year sentence at this college, I still can't write about these experiences without anger and frustration seeping through my pen.

The incidents continue as I feel all eyes are watching my every move.

One afternoon, Lindley, a black girl from Detroit, and Todd, a white friend from our hall, and I go in to town. On our way back from grocery shopping we notice a bunch of milk crates behind the grocery store in an alley. We pull over and fill the car with the crates thinking they will make great additions to our rooms. We each take three or four crates and return to our dorms. Within 15 minutes the police are at our door. Someone saw us taking the crates and called the police. They got Todd's license plate number and they traced it back to his dad, who happened to be a professor at the college. The interesting things is that the police showed up at our door first, not Todd's. Somewhere the police had to inquire about two black students and were directed to our room. The police tell us to call everyone involved to our room and once everyone arrived the police collect the crates and lecture us on how bad it is to steal. Lindley and I didn't consider this stealing. If you left something like this out behind a store in an alley in Detroit or New York it was trash.

When this story is told as an isolated incident, it is easy to see the misunderstanding and many would argue this is all it was; just a misunderstanding. It would be hard for me to prove them wrong. So I am left to ponder if it is me or if it is them. Am I too sensitive? Am I the crazy one? Am I looking at life through a lens that needs to be corrected? It causes me to question myself. It causes me to question my actions. It causes me to be afraid to take another step for fear I will step into another "misunderstanding." I had inherited my Dad's affliction. Every situation now had the potential to be racial.

This small private college was not overtly hostile. I wasn't aware of groups that gathered to talk about white supremacy. There was never a time where I was attacked because I was black. But the environment was not openly welcoming. It was obvious to me the college didn't know how to address these subtle issues so they ignored them which made me feel ignored. The fact that I had only one other person who saw things as I did was maddening.

Dating in college is a new experience. I joke that I am an equal opportunity employer stating I will date any race as long as they look good. My sophomore year I date my first white girl, a girl from Naperville, Illinois. Prior to us going out I met her parents. They are president of the parents association. They are quirky folks but a lot of fun. Everyone loves them. They are very active around the college and visit often. They show up at Halloween and her father is dressed as a cheerleader and her mother is dressed as a football player. They make the rounds through all the dorms trick or treating and even go to some of the frat parties. They are seen as the coolest parents at the college.

The spring following their Halloween appearance, I begin dating their daughter. She is goofy, and silly, and a little smothering, but she helps my four year sentence at college pass. She is more into us than I am and she can't wait to tell her parents about us.

She calls me over to her room one night and she is in tears, sobbing uncontrollably. Through her sobs she tells me she has told her parents about us. As she calms down, she notices she is getting no comfort from me. She goes on to explain to me how they took the news. Her father can do nothing but sit at the kitchen table and cry. Her mother says nothing. Her silence sends a strong message. This is heartbreaking to see my potential presence in their family has caused these likeable people to be so unlikeable.

A few weeks later it is parents' weekend and we are still dating. My enthusiasm for the relationship has waned but it is better than spending time alone. Her mother is still not talking and refuses to come to parents' weekend despite the fact that she and her husband are head of the group sponsoring the weekend. She can't bear to see her daughter with a black boy. Her father comes and I refuse to meet him.

I have to work in the cafeteria as part of my financial aid package and to survive. As I am working she and her father walk into the cafeteria and our eyes meet. He makes a weak attempt at being friendly and I picture this man sitting at a kitchen table weeping. My respect for him is gone and I make no attempt at all. I walk by him as if he is not there.

She is heart broken and I am annoyed. She goes to talk to a campus counselor and the counselor requests that I come back with her. This is the weight that tilts the relationship/work scale. This relationship is too much work and I do not care to devote that kind of energy into this insanity. I end the relationship and pity their family.

My junior year I meet a girl from Grand Rapids, Michigan. She went to a more diverse high school and through our conversations I can tell she is more comfortable around blacks. She sells me on the "my best friend at home is black argument." She is nice, attractive and again time goes by quicker with company. She grew up with her mother who was a single parent and her growing up was a struggle. She is not part of the privileged group that dominates this campus. We date for about six months and on a break from school she asks me to come home and meet her mother. As we pull into the driveway, the phone in the house rings. The girl's grandfather who lives nearby has been in a car accident. He and his wife are at the hospital but will soon be released and taken home stiff and sore.

We turn around and head to their house about 30 minutes away. In 30 minutes I get to meet the entire family including an uncle, who my date has told me fought in Viet Nam, is half crazy, and hates black people because of something that happened between him and some black soldiers in Viet Nam. I also get to meet an Aunt who is liberal minded and I am told will like me.

We arrive at her grandfather's home. Soon he arrives with a bruised and bandaged forehead and all the kids and grandkids trip over each other to show their concern. He is not a warm grandfather at all. They all cater to him to stay in his favor. They are all afraid of him and he controls the family in a scary kind of way.

We are introduced and he extends a hand that is limp and fish-like. I shake it and he says nothing to me. Instinctively, I want to pull out my family portrait and show him I have some ties to white people but I quickly accept that there is nothing I can do that will make him like me. I meet the uncle, the war veteran, and I cut the conversation short. My fear is I will say or do something that will cause him to flash back to Vietnam and he will begin spitting out racial slurs that could make a trucker blush.

I meet the aunt and she is friendly and I direct all my attention to her and my girlfriend when she isn't catering to her grandfather's every need. My girlfriend is noticeably one of her grandfather's favorites but our being together does not hold his attention or get his blessing. I slowly watch the clock praying to God this uncomfortable meeting will end soon.

We continue to date for over a year and some at college are all right with it and some of her friends are noticeably uncomfortable with us. Several of her friends spend their time whispering in her ear telling her she can do better than me. They are on constant watch just waiting for me to prove them right. Their hatred for me is unfounded but very aggressive and I am constantly retracing my steps to see what it is that I did to set them off. While in the middle of this character assassination the obvious escapes me. Their motivation finally rings a bell in my ever vigilant mind after several months of them shooting venom in my direction.

As I inch closer to graduation, I realize I will be leaving soon and fantasize about the black women I will meet when I go back to Detroit. The reception of my black friends back in Detroit also concerns me when they hear I am dating a white girl. In anticipation of this fantasy and in fear of ridicule I end the relationship for no legitimate reason. In the end, I decide interracial relationships are too much work. I am not strong enough to wage the war and prove to the world why interracial relationships are all right and I don't have the desire to fight the world every time we go out.

College is a bitter but necessary experience for me. It is like swallowing medicine that tastes like dirt. The act of forcing the medicine down is painful, but digesting the medicine will make my future more tolerable. I am given a huge dose of the real world and it is overwhelming. The loss of control is devastating. In Detroit, I was a part-time minority. I knew when and where to expect to be treated differently. At college, I am a minority everyday, all day. Daily I miss those who are like me, those that understand me. I also miss the likeable me. This change in environment is such a shock to my system that my personality changes and I become someone *I* don't even like.

Throughout my four years I do make several white friends and their companionship is welcomed. The shame is I could have made so many more good friends but I made it impossible to see them over my self-constructed wall. The struggle for me was identifying the right ones to let in and how to keep the wrong ones out. I was convinced those that I did get to know had the potential to betray me behind closed doors with racist remarks and attitudes. Moving though college was like walking through a minefield scared that my next step could end in an explosion I would never hear. This fear created a lonely four years. The confusing part was that this fear was sometimes accurate and often times just my own paranoia.

I regret that the shade of black that I chose to show was the shade so many of my white friends had seen on TV and in the movies. The shade of black I regret I didn't show was a shade that is not what is expected. The three dimensional shades with tones and hues that showed more than what society markets is what I should've shown. I chose to protect myself and shut down, cheating everyone around me. At that age, I didn't have the energy to speak for an entire race.

My tutelage in the "us" versus "them" mentality saves me. Instead of taking on the burden that it is me who is deficient, this mentality told me it is "them." The pride in my race propped me up and allowed me to withstand the exclusion and oppression. This pride protected my outer shell but my internal wounds do not heal so quickly. I manage to survive but some internal gashes left scars that I am still nursing.

Experiencing this environment bonds me to those heroes in the past that endured much more. Prior to college real oppression was in a textbook that had no feeling attached to it. Going through it and its invisible effects strengthens me.

College helps me to understand the sacrifices that Mom and Dad made to protect me from this realization earlier in my life. Although it is a shock to my system, it comes at a time where I am mature enough to handle it. The four year degree I receive in real life becomes more valuable than the bachelors degree I receive in the spring of 1989. This is not the only priceless lesson I learn while at college.

17

MOTHER?

Are you my mother?

There is a Dr. Seuss book called, *Are you My Mother?* It is the story of a little bird that hatches when his mother is away from the nest. The bird then sets out to find his mother. He goes up to animal after animal and simple asks, "Are you my mother?"

Off and on I feel like that bird. I want to walk up to women and just ask, "Are you my mother?" It is my fantasy that after a few negative responses, I will find my mother and she will deliver a worm to me and hug me just like mother bird does to the baby bird in the book.

Growing up I always wondered about my biological mother. The thoughts of wonder led to fantasies about my mother being rich and her coming to find me. I'd imagine when she located me she'd give me a big basket full of money. She'd then leave me with Mom and Dad but check up on me every now and then to drop off a new basket of money each time.

If she isn't rich, she is famous. I imagine I am the descendant of royalty. British royalty or Hollywood royalty, it doesn't matter. Then I wonder what I would sound like with a British accent or how I would look in a big Hollywood mansion. My stream of consciousness takes me on a wild ride down a river that eventually is on the opposite side of the earth far away from mother thoughts.

My mother thoughts never leave me but they do not consume me either. On special occasions like Christmas or my birthday I wonder if she is out there and what she is thinking about. The emotions I have for her are hard to describe. I do not miss her because I never had her. It is more of a haunting curiosity. My vivid imagination soars through time and space occasionally, hovering over her to just watch how she interacts and moves through life. The thought of being close but invisible is soothing. Direct interaction is terrifying.

In college I decide to venture out and see if I can find my mother. The solitude of college gives me the courage to try to stitch together fantasy and reality.

Through the phone I can hear her leaf through the pages of my file. She gives very short answers to my long questions. The most common answer I get is, "I'm sorry I can't tell you that."

On the other end of the phone is the woman from the private adoption agency. I sit at my desk in my dorm room and I can picture my file. I imagine it to be three to four inches thick and pregnant with papers, notes, reports and information about me. It is often said people go away to college to "find themselves" and I am attempting to do just that.

Being away from home I realize the sacrifices Mom and Dad have made for me and it heightens the sense of family and closeness I have for them. This idea of family makes we wonder about my birth parents and the circumstances that caused them to give me up for adoption. The wonder is concentrated on my birth mother. For reasons I can't explain, my father is of some interest but my mother is the treasure I seek.

My fantasy continues about the woman who created me and what she is like now and what she was like when she gave me up. I hesitate to pursue her because I am not sure her reality will match my fantasy.

I am also hesitant because I don't want Mom and Dad to feel slighted. The urge to protect them and their feelings is very powerful and part of me thinks if I go looking for my birth parents I will somehow betray the ones that have loved me unconditionally.

I call home to Mom and Dad. I tell them how college is going and for the first time ever I ask questions about my adoption. I hold my breath as I ask what agency handled my adoption.

The research I have done to this point tells me that this is the first place to start my journey. On the other end of the phone, Mom and Dad explode. It is like they are just waiting for me to ask. They download to me years and years of information and give me the name of the private adoption agency that handled my adoption. They explain to me the circumstances around my adoption and anything they can remember. I hang up the phone relieved and I am certain they do too.

The next day I place a call to the adoption agency in Detroit. I am transferred to the woman assigned to my file. I give her my name and birth date and she asks me to hold on. I imagine her going to a large filing cabinet and pulling out my file. She returns to the phone and I begin to ask questions about my birthparents. The shuffling of paper begins. She tells me that my birth mother did not sign a consent form. The consent form would allow me access to the file the caseworker holds in her hands. Since there is no consent form in the file, my access is denied. This frustrates me because technically my birth mother did not say I could not see the information. She never said either way but since this one piece of paper is not in the file my birth mother's right to privacy trumps my right to my own information.

This thought plays over and over in my head. I am sitting on my desk in the corner of my dorm room and I am talking to a woman in Detroit. She, who has no connection to me, knows more about me than I do. The name of my birth parents, and their social security numbers, are all on a desk in Detroit and I can't see it. I sit at college powerless. There is no arguing this and it appears my search has ended before it begins.

As a consolation, the woman informs me that she can send me my "non-identifying information." She explains this is information about my birth parents that is just that, non-identifying. I want to scream and yell and chew this woman's head off. She is only doing her job but I want to flood her ear with the injustice that I feel about this system. Fortunately, my rational side knows she doesn't have the power to do anything different. The phrase, "A bird in the hand, a bird in the hand" rings in my head.

I resign to giving her my address at school and I ask her politely to send me what she can and thank her for her assistance.

An eternity passes over the next two weeks and I wait for the paperwork to come. Finally, it arrives. I open the envelope and there in seconds I learn more about myself than I ever knew.

I am the son of a white woman and black man. He was a cook and she was a cafeteria worker. They worked at one of the major auto companies in Detroit. They were married, but to other people.

This was a screwball I did not see coming. I always assumed they were two young kids who got caught in the moment. The fact that I was the result of an affair is shocking. Over the years, my imagination filled in the blanks and I was not even close. I painted the picture of two teenagers who had me and then went their separate ways.

The idea of having brothers and sisters was never drawn up in the sketch I'd created of my birth family. In these two pages I find out I have three brothers and one sister from my birth mother's marriage. My birth father also had children but it doesn't say how many. They are both still married at the time of my birth; neither planned to leave their spouses.

My creative mind imagines the conversation my birth mother had with her husband about me and I am sure it was a colorful one.

The information is the least I learn. The conversation I had with myself over the years about these two strangers and who they are surprises me. I assumed I did not give it much thought, but to see my reactions to the truth tells me I put a lot of thought in to it.

My interest again is concentrated on my birth mother. I learn she is 5'1' and just over one hundred pounds when I was born. She has blond hair and blue eyes; that makes me laugh. I am the son of a blond hair and blue eyed woman; again, not what I pictured. I want to see what she looks likes, hear how she sounds, see if any of her mannerisms were passed on to me. For the first time I realize a foreign thought. There is someone out there that looks like me. After years of being the different one I comprehend the thought that there is someone who shares my DNA.

My creative mind continues to digest this new information and begins writing a new script. My story is now that my birth mother had me and continued living. The children were too young to remember and her husband ignores this bump in the road but never forgets. The auto company rendezvous' and the resulting pregnancy are never mentioned again. I fade away like a bad phase my birth mother went through. To her, I am "Out of sight, out of mind."

Since I can't connect with those that know the truth I make it up. The desire is still in me to get the full truth from those that created me. I want to know why I was put up for adoption and I want to know the real story behind the standard answer I've heard all my life.

"Your mother couldn't take care of you and wanted you to have a better life."

I have never known what that is supposed to mean.

The letter is folded and I store it with my memory book Mom gave me when I graduated from high school. I call Mom and Dad and I tell them what the letter says and they are excited to hear about what we never knew. They are happy that I got to fill in some of the blanks. Dad encourages me to try and find my birth mother. I tell him my search has come to a road block. I received all the information I am allowed. Dad tells me to look her up by her last name in the phone book. I feel like I am having a conversation with a child. "Dad, they will not give me her name. That is part of the identifying information I don't have access to." Dad responds: "On your original birth certificate I think you were listed as, baby boy Pervine. There can't be a whole lot of Pervines in Detroit."

I am shocked. Now I have a last name that I either didn't hear or that was left out in our first adoption conversation. Dad says it like everyone knows it. "Wasn't that it?" my Dad says to Mom who is on the other phone in the house. "Yes, I think you're right."

It is not much but it gives a faint heartbeat to my search. The next day I make a call back to the adoption agency. My caseworker grabs my file and again I hear the maddening turning of paper. I ask her if she could tell me my birth mother's name. Before I finish the sentence I know her answer, "I am sorry I can not give you that information." We have been through this before and I am sure she has been through this with many, many adoptees. She is so rehearsed in it that she can say it with if no feeling or compassion at all.

The conversation goes quiet between us and I am searching my mind to get any more information I can out of her. I blurt out, "My parents told me her last name is Pervine. How do you spell that?" Desperation is intertwined with my words and the conversation goes quiet. She has turned down the temperature of her cold heart. She is just not going to answer my question. After a few more seconds she says very professionally, "As per our earlier conversation, I cannot give you that information." I don't respond. She repeats what she just said. "As *per* our earlier conversation. I cannot give you that information."

She is giving me a clue and I am missing it. My desperation thawed her heart. "So it is P-E-R-V-I-N-E right?"

Quietly she says, "Yes. Is there anything else I can help you with?"

"Nope, that is it. Thank you very much." I hang up the phone.

I search for Pervine in the Detroit area and don't have any luck. The desire to find out more surprisingly and quickly subsides. The idea of busting into a family that probably knows nothing about me is not very appealing. The fact that I now have a last name satisfies my immediate appetite. I end my search with some blanks filled in and a new story I have created that has a more realistic explanation.

My search does not end with a worm and a hug but I am satisfied. The memory book that holds my information is packed away and the urgency to dig for my lost treasure is replaced by the need to digest what I have learned. In the back corner of my mind, I will occasionally pick up this information and toss it around. Periodically, I toy with the idea and hope that somewhere in the Detroit area there is a blond hair and blue eyed woman who is searching for me and my story of being gone and forgotten is not close to the truth.

For now fantasy still replaces reality again and I am satisfied, but the possibility of what I might find or who might find me is exciting.

18

HOME AGAIN?

In May of 1989, I leave college and I am grateful for the mind-expanding experience and more grateful it is now over.

My studies in college went well despite the fact that I chose and stayed with the wrong major. I entered college with the hopes of becoming a Physical Therapist and majored in Exercise Physiology. Chemistry class and Genetics class very quickly killed that hope. I struggled with the course work in my major but breezed through the course work in my minor, English. During my senior year it occurred me, I probably should have majored in English. Fortunately, I did well enough to secure an internship at St. Joseph Hospital in Ann Arbor Michigan with their cardiac rehabilitation department. Although this is not my initial goal it is a chance at a viable career.

My plan is to go home to Mom and Dad in Ohio where they have landed finally with a church that Dad pastors in a small rural town. It is interesting what door opens once the black kid is away at college. I will spend the summer there and then leave to go to Ann Arbor to start my internship in the fall.

The combination of small town and my newfound independence don't mix well. The leap from Detroit to this rural town is painful. I have finally been paroled from college/prison and this small town doesn't have the excitement I need. Again I struggle with making new friends and the black population is close to nonexistent in this little farm town.

The shift from being on my own to under my parents roof is stifling. We all enjoyed our freedom the last four years and I can't go back to "My rules, my house." I spend two or three weeks with my parents and realize I have got to go for the betterment of the family and my sanity.

I place a call to Detroit, to Mrs. Tenbusch, my best friend's mom who lived across the street from us on Shaftsbury Street. I ask if I can stay there until my fall internship begins. I am welcomed back just as I expect. I inherit John's room, which is now empty as John stayed in Chicago after he graduated from college. Mike and Mollie are away at college and Joey, who has grown up to become Joe, is the last child at home.

To this point, I have had a decent relationship with Joe. He is six years younger than me so as I grew up I did not spend too much time with him. He is a friend by association through Mike.

Joe is now 15 and submersed in high school. We spend the summer together playing basketball and lifting weights in between my work schedule. Joe is a respectful, quiet, and thoughtful 15 year old who is on the verge of finding his comfortable place in teenage life.

We sit in the basement watching rap videos and playing video games hour after hour and talking about everything and nothing. Joe is a scholar when it comes to the Civil Rights Movement. He knows far more than I do about great black leaders, and Detroit's history. I adopt Joe as the younger brother I never had or wanted and I cherish our new friendship.

Jose is still living next door with his mom while he attends a local college in the Detroit area. Mr. Galano passed away while I was at college. The bitter taste and thoughts I had for Mr. Galano are totally dissolved well before Mr. Galano dies. Over the years, the Galanos have become part of my extended family.

It is good to be home, blasting the radio set to WJLB, the biggest black radio station in Detroit, and playing basketball with these two guys who transformed into brothers over the years. No longer do I have to question the intentions of those around me. Once again, I breathe in calm and allow myself to relax. I fit in again even though I am surrounded by white people. I can just be me and finding this place at this time of my life is priceless.

During this summer, I can't find a steady job, so I hire on as a "Kelly girl" with Kelly Temporary services. The lack of funds easily washes away pride. I spend May and most of June doing temp jobs in and around Detroit. I quickly learn I can't do this for too much longer.

In mid-June I learn the internship I thought started in September starts in two weeks, and I have no place to stay in Ann Arbor. I extend my stay with the Tenbuschs through December and commute to St. Joseph's which is 45 minutes away.

The internship is my first exposure to the real work force. I shadow the cardiac technicians who run the cardiac rehab classes for those fresh from cardiac surgery. I also watch and assist with stress tests. Soon I learn this really isn't my type of work. As I watch the cardiac technicians, set up, administer and complete the stress tests, running up to twelve in one hour, I realize the scales are uneven. They are paid not much more than minimum wage and the Cardiologist who sticks his head in occasionally gets paid a six figure salary. I grow to detest the Cardiologists who are very pompous and condescending to everyone. The internship clearly teaches me what I *don't* want to grow up to be in life.

My first exposure to adult work life is an easy transition. College has prepared me well so I expect to be the only black where I work and it is not a shock when my expectations are met. The anger and bitterness that I had in college doesn't follow home or to work and I am able to function and socialize easily. The comfort of knowing I can retreat to Shaftsbury Street at the end of the day where I am understood creates a happier me.

Playing the work game comes easy. I quickly realize I must function differently at work than I do at home. Thanks to all of my growing pains this can be done like the flip of a switch. I know to talk proper while at work.(finally, talking proper has its advantages). I know to present myself at work more polished and articulate. When I exit work on the ride home I can blast my rap music and relax. While with my friends, I strap on my tongue that speaks slang and talk in a way that would be incomprehensible at work. This double life of switching back and forth is a necessary part of functioning in the work world and a priceless gift to comprehend. I know many black friends that are unable to switch back and forth and success in the work world is impossible for many unless you flip the switch. If I had understood the need to do so in college I would have faired much better.

In December as my internship ends, I send my resume out and begin looking for a job. My plan is to stay in Detroit, the city that is such a comfort to me. I search and search and I can't find a job. I return as a Kelly girl just to have *some* money.

I know it is time to move on and out of the Tenbusch basement. Mrs. T. would let me stay there forever but it was time to try and fly on my own. I only need a descent job to support me and I can find nothing.

One day when there is no temporary work, I go down to the MESC (Michigan Employment Security Commission) office. This is a service to help the unemployed find employment. I go and stand in a line that wraps around the outside of the building with my shirt and tie on and a handful of resumes. Finally inside the building I am directed to a line to register. I wait in that line, fill out the necessary paperwork and I am sent to another line. In this line, I wait to take some kind of test. This test will help me determine what kind of job I should be doing. After I finish the test, I am allowed to sit down and wait for an employment professional to call my name so we can discuss my future.

I sit in the back of the room and look around. Despair descends on me like fog. There are professionals in suits, young mothers with small children, and blue collar workers dressed in working man coveralls, and we are all looking, praying, pleading for work.

Behind the counters, in front of the many lines, are the people who have jobs. On the floor in front of the counter at the beginning of the lines is tape. The rules are clear. You don't step over this tape until you get the signal from the worker behind the counter. It is amazing to see the different signals used to call people forward. Once the person at the counter who is being helped walks away, the next person in line looks up hopefully. If you are fortunate you get the immediate head nod. Those that are more cautious will wait for the second head nod to confirm they actually saw the first head nod.

Typically, what happens is the last person walks away and the worker behind the counter avoids all eye contact with the next person in line. The worker will shuffle papers, restack papers, organize paper clips, refile and unfile folders and concentrate on selling the idea that they are busier than the President of The

United States. I can't figure out how telling person after person you have no work for them can generate this much paperwork.

All compassion and empathy has long since drained from the faces of the workers. They don't like their jobs and it is evident by the way they do their jobs. I find some sad humor in this because, given the chance, there is a room full of people that would exchange positions with those on the other side of the sacred counter. We would jump at the opportunity to lose all compassion and empathy for those without jobs.

I initially rest my head against the back wall and then unconsciously began slowly hitting my head against it. This room is closing in on me and extracting my hope. I follow protocol and wait for my name to be called. I go up to find out there are no positions for me. They tell me to come back in a few weeks to see if any new positions are available. I leave the office and resolve I can never go back.

Slowly, I am coming to the realization that Detroit is not what I hoped it would be for me. On the way back to Shaftsbury, I reflect back on the Detroit I loved so much. On Shaftsbury over the past 14 years reality has slowly crept in and taken up residence.

I remember the murder of the woman I used to deliver the paper to just two blocks from my house that occurred while I was in grade school. She went to have work done on her car at a local garage. They were going to have to keep the car over night so one of the mechanics offered to drive her home. When the mechanic dropped her off, he followed her in to the house and killed her. Her son found his mother in the kitchen when he came home from school that day.

There was the cop who moved in to Peter's house who *accidently* shot his girlfriend in the pelvis while cleaning his gun. She lived, the relationship didn't, and he was never charged.

In that same house, after the cop moved away, a single father and his two teenage daughters moved in while I am in high school. I become friends with the younger sister and spend hours talking and joking with her. The older sister had a baby with her boyfriend shortly before I leave for college. While I am away at college, the boyfriend storms into the house and shoots and kills his girlfriend in the upstairs hallway, and also shoots my friend before he exits the house. Fortunately the baby is not harmed.

My friend survives and takes on the responsibility of raising her nephew as his father is sent to prison.

The quiet street I grew to love is getting louder and louder. The city I so keenly defended to the sheltered whites in college is getting harder and harder to endorse. The city that I fit so well in no longer fits what I want out of life.

On the ride back to Shaftsbury after my MESC experience I make a decision. I would at least look into Mom's advice and call the headhunter in Toledo, Ohio, a much smaller, calmer city sixty miles south of Detroit. Mom had been trying subtly to get me out of Detroit because her parental vision saw what I refused to see.

I call the headhunter and meet with her in her small second floor office in downtown Toledo. She is patient and calm and committed to finding me a job. After a few trips back and forth from Detroit to Toledo, she finds me a great lead on a job with an insurance company, as a claims adjuster. The starting salary is $23,000. Up to this point, the best salary rate I ever made was $10,000 a year. I have no idea what a claims adjuster does, but I am certain I will be a good one.

I fill out the application and remember that since I couldn't put my race on the application and my last name is misleading, that I had to somehow identify myself as a minority. On my resume, under interests I simple put: Member of the NAACP. I am desperate and if my color can help me, I am sure going to use it. I figure it is about time my color is an advantage.

The interview goes very well. So does the second interview. Then I have to sit and wait. At my temp jobs in Detroit I am praying I will return home to find a message from the insurance company. Finally, the phone rings and I am moving to Toledo.

Leaving Detroit is sweet with a bitter aftertaste. This city has given me such pride and has helped raise me. The history of the city has had an amazing effect on who I am and now I leave it to find something better knowing I will have to live as a minority again. I grieve the loss of comfort but I am hopeful and excited about finding a better balance. I am confident, after my college experience I can function in any environment. Maybe Toledo will have something I couldn't find in Detroit.

19

FINALLY ANSWERED

Bending over in front of me, behind the counter of Fifth Third Bank is a very cute bank teller. The bank is a mile from my new apartment and I have found an excuse to come in almost everyday. The bank shares space inside the Kroger grocery store at Spring Meadows mall in Toledo, Ohio. I come in frequently, and I take out five to ten dollars. Once this is spent I return and do it again.

Since I'm new to the area, finding young women my age to talk to me is not easy. I am guaranteed when I come in that she will speak to me, if she is free. She has to talk to me; this is her job. I notice her amazing full lips and deep dimples the first time I come to the bank. The dimples and lips are as if God himself drew them on her.

She is friendly and I can't tell if it is because she has to be or because she wants to be. Her nametag reads, Shilease.

My skills with women need a lot of work. I have learned early in life that I may not be the coolest and most dashing fellow, but if I get the chance to speak and can show my charm and sense of humor, that makes up for my un-Denzel-like appearance. The challenge has always been getting up the courage to start the conversation.

I was introduced to my current girlfriend who lives in Detroit by a close high school friend, which made things much easier for me. Since my move I only see her on the weekends and my weeks are long and lonely. The fact that I am lonely helps justify my desire to talk to the teller in front of me.

Watching this petite young lady behind the counter sends a surge of courage through my veins. My body has decided before my brain that I am going to have to find a way to ask this young lady out.

Distracted by her tight purple suede mini skirt, I try to complete my deposit slip but my eyes keep drifting to see more purple suede. She turns around and quickly I divert my eyes to my paperwork hoping she did not see me looking at her nice curvy mini-skirt.

Her smile is electric and my courage surges again. I cannot speak because the pounding of my heart in my ears is deafening. She takes my deposit, I thank her, and I walk away, dazed. My transactions over the past few months have only involved seeing her from her tiny waist up. This is the first time I see more of her. It is such a shock to me I totally forget to withdrawal any money. The embarrassment of returning today is too much for my system to handle. I will come back tomorrow.

Since high school, I have dated pretty regularly. After the experiences I had in college with dating I concluded that the added hassle involved with dating someone from another race just wasn't worth it. It is not something I am against for others, but my shoulders are not broad enough to bear that cross.

There is one other reason why I have gravitated to black girls. Ever since I noticed girls in school the emphasis was always on their shapely figures. Besides color, this is the biggest difference in cultures that I have experienced. The black community celebrates the women with the more curvy figures. If you are a black girl with no hips you lose the attention to the black girl with hips. This is the polar opposite of the white culture. If you are white and have too many curves you are considered fat and generally less desirable.

Growing up, the only girls I came in contact with on a regular basis were the black girls in school. I grew up being attracted to more shapely black girls.

My teller at the bank is black, very attractive and after I saw her bend over I realize she fills the last requirement as well. Now how am I going to harness the courage to ask her out? I have not found an answer to that question before I return the next day to withdrawal money so I can eat.

I'm waiting in line and see her perfect smile and beautiful lips as she speaks politely to customers ahead of me. I think she looks up and smiles at me but I am unsure. I am standing in line doing Lamaze techniques to try and slow down my heart so I can hear and speak. I start counting off customers to see if she will wait on me.

"Ok, if this guy in front of me is quick and the customer at the other window takes a little longer I should get Shilease." I think to myself.

God smiles on me and it goes as planned. The customer in front of me makes a quick deposit and is gone. I step to the window and before I can push something out, that I pray is English, she speaks.

"You're lucky I am your teller."

I know. Thank you Jesus! I think to myself but I say nothing. I smile and she continues.

"I checked your deposit and you wrote the wrong account number on your deposit slip yesterday. Don't worry, I changed it." She says.

I love how your dimples and lips move when you talk, I say to myself.

I graciously thank her and withdraw my usual five dollars. As she is processing my request, we make small talk and I swear she is flirting with me, but I'm not certain. I thank her again for correcting my mistake and I leave trying to think of what I will say when I return tomorrow for another five dollars.

On my way home something occurs to me. I remember, from being a teller on my summer breaks during college, that there is no reason for a teller to check someone's deposit slip. When you take in a deposit, you attach the deposit slip to the check and put it in your out box. Later, the check and deposit slip get sent down to the proof department. The errors are caught in the proof department *NOT* at the teller window. So why was she studying my deposit slip so closely?

Remembering back to my teller days, I recall my process if a cute girl came in to the bank. I would hold her paperwork to the side and when I got a chance later I would use the paperwork to look up her information. There I could find out if she was married, who else was on the account, and how old she was.

Is this what Shilease is doing? Was she checking me out?
She *was* flirting with me!

I only need a little encouragement to act. I am tired of playing
"What if." Passing my apartment, I head straight for the florist.
I send a bouquet of flowers directly to the bank addressed to
Shilease. I attach a card that reads, "Thanks for correcting my
mistakes. Call me. Kevin Hofmann" Then I wrote my number.
Again my heart is racing and testosterone is doing laps in my
veins. I am in such a hurry to do this because I fear the courage
will retreat. My haste causes me to miss the fact that I wrote my
phone number wrong and don't realize it.

Returning home I juggle back and forth in my mind whether
I should have sent the flowers or not. The relief of finally doing
something is attacked by the preoccupation that I may have read
the situation wrong. I conclude; this will force an answer good
or bad. Tomorrow will deliver the answer.

After I finish dinner, and watch some TV in my small
apartment, I decide to go to bed early. Sleep will make tomorrow
come sooner. Before I go to bed, I call my girlfriend in Detroit.
The conversation is cut short because I can't concentrate on
two women at once. "The long day has worn me out." is my
excuse and I cut the nightly talk short and go to bed. The guilt
I harbor in my chest also makes it uncomfortable to talk to the
unsuspecting girl in Detroit.

My eight hour work day seems like a week. Finally, I am
dismissed and I hurry home to check my answering machine.
The machine is empty. I check all cords and make sure there is
nothing wrong with the phone mechanically. I check to make
sure there is a tape in the machine also. There is a tape in the
machine.

She has not called.

Tomorrow, I will have to find another bank. What I thought
was a straight fastball, was a curve. I swung for the rooftop and
hit nothing but air. My pride is damaged and I comfort myself by
telling myself I still have a girlfriend in Detroit.

As I am fixing my usual entree for dinner, cream-style corn,
and I am dancing to the music from my portable stereo (I am
a great dancer alone in my apartment), I reassure myself that

Shilease let one get away. My confidence is just about back to "full" when the phone rings.

I freeze.

The corn is bubbling in the pot, the music is loud and the phone is on the second ring. I have to turn down the stove, turn off the music and get to the phone in the living room in two rings before the machine picks up. For the first time, I am thankful my apartment is so small. In one leap, the stove and radio are off and I am diving to the phone.

"Hello?" Calm is how I hope I sound, but desperate and out if breath is probably more accurate.

"Hi, this is Shilease from the bank. Thank you for my flowers."

She sounds great on the phone!

"Thanks for taking care of those mistakes for me." I say, able to regain some composure.

"You put the wrong phone number on the card. I had to look up your correct number." She cares enough to look up the right number. YES!!

The conversation flows easy and smooth. After about ten minutes of good conversation, my self-esteem has been restored and I can tell I read the situation right.

Confidently, I say, "So where are we going to go tomorrow after you get off work?" I hold my breath hoping that is as smooth as I thought it would be. She answers without a pause.

"I don't know. Where do you want to go?"

She sounds great on the phone!

"How about the movies? We can go see *Harlem Nights* with Eddie Murphy."

"That would be fine." She says.

Touch down! Home run! Extra point! Field goal!

We begin to see each other regularly. I spend as much time as I can with her. Her easy personality is great. She is smart, kind and quick to put me in check. I like that.

Weeks dissolve into months and we continue to see each other Monday through Thursday. On Friday, I pack up and go to Detroit to see my girlfriend and friends back in Detroit. I like the attention I get through dating and always have. There is something about dating that fills me up inside. To date two women at the same time is hectic and the guilt that I feel nags at me. I try to push it away but when I am alone the guilt sneaks up on me. The attention feeds my ego and being wanted by two women fills a hole in me and artificially inflates my self-esteem. For now the need to be liked out weighs the guilt.

Shilease and I met in May of 1990 and by August of that same year the guilt of running back and forth begins to tip the scales. I come clean and tell Shilease about the girl in Detroit.

Casually, she says, "I know." She is hurt, but her confident ways tells her not to show it.

We continue Monday through Thursday and I think since nothing more is said that it is ok. My ego convinces me to only respond when Shilease calls. I stop calling her and my cool nonchalant attitude when she does call is rude at best.

Suddenly, the messages that used to be there when I come home from Detroit aren't there. Shilease stops calling. She cuts me off, no explanation and Shilease disappears. The relationship I thought I had total control over was unraveling. After several weeks of being without this light in my life, I put my ego in the hallway and call Shilease.

"Hey, how are you? Are your fingers broken? How come you don't call me anymore?" I calmly say.

I don't hear what she says back. The fact that she is still talking to me is a great relief. The message is clear. She won't take my crap. I like that.

It is now late fall and although my trips to Detroit are still happening they are happening less and less. The need to fill this deficiency in me is still there and I am unwilling to cut off one of the sources feeding me. Shilease and I spend all our free time together and I enjoy her company.

As Christmas comes and goes, someone speaks to me. In a rare instance when I am alone in my apartment, I hear a voice say, "She is so nice to you. Why do you treat her so cruelly?"

Although, I have been nicer to her than I was a few months ago, I am still seeing the girl in Detroit. I am aware Shilease has feelings for me, but I am still seeing the girl in Detroit. In an instant, I know the answer and what I must do.

I make a final trip to Detroit and end the relationship. I finally act on a decision I should have made several months ago.

When I return to Toledo, I go over to Shilease's house, explain I have ended the relationship in Detroit and beg her to forgive me. We decide to start things fresh and I thank God for her.

We are now inseparable. I pick her up from work and bring her to my apartment. We see each other Sunday through Saturday. The only time we don't see each other is when we are working.

I introduce her to the Detroit family and to Mom and Dad and she is brought into both families.

We date for another six months and we talk about getting married. At this point we have been together for over a year. We decide we are ready and we will get engaged soon. I just don't tell her when or where.

By now Shilease has a key to my apartment. I tell her I am going out after work and ask her to stop by after she gets off work. She knows she will be there before me.

While she is at work I buy two dozen silk white roses. I make a path from the front door to the dining room table. On the table is the ring box. Shilease comes in and follows the rose path to the dining room table. As she gets to the table and sees the ring box I step out of the bedroom dressed in my best suit.

"You didn't think I wouldn't be here to ask you this did you? Will you marry me?" I softly ask.

"Yes" she softly says back. She sounds good.

We arrange to get married in 16 months. We take the time to plan and organize and arrange and get to know each other.

In September of 1993, we get married. The left side of the church is her friends and family, mostly all black. On the right side of the church are my friends and family, mostly all white. Mike and Joe are beside me when Shilease and I get married.

Over the next two years we struggle, both financially and as a young married couple. We somehow get a bank to loan us money and we buy a house in a black neighborhood and soon after Shilease is pregnant. She gets bigger and more beautiful with each day and she puts up with an immature husband who never knows the right thing to say or do.

In 1996 we have our first son, Tai Malik

Finally, there is someone in my family who has part of me in them.

He is a well-behaved baby. He is thoughtful and investigates everything with his eyes. He makes parenting an ease and a joy.

I later find out giving me a blood relative is a present Shilease was anxious to give me. It is a powerful moment for me in ways that most take for granted. Our son is light skinned like me and a piece of my incomplete puzzle.

Four years later his brother, Zion Mekhi is born. He is the polar opposite of his quiet brother. Our new son investigates with his hands. This often leads to a mess or something broken. He teaches me patience. He has Shilease's skin tone and her perfect round head.

Again I share DNA with someone I know. When I sit and feed my sons or pick them up I wonder what their biological grandmother would say. She can't help but love them. They are adorable.

I envision the day I will introduce them to her. She still runs through my thoughts and every now and then I dance with the fantasy of her. Seeing my own sons I realize this meeting will have to be attempted. I have a desire for her to see my boys. She would be so proud.

The idea of her being proud is a new idea, but deep under my heart is a need for her to be proud of me. I want her to be relieved that the choice she made was a good one and I turned out all right. The search for her is not over. The seed of desire is planted again, and this time is has a few extra branches. The particulars of when I will search for her again are not yet pressing.

My move to Toledo fills many holes and creates a scenario for even more to be filled.

20

JOURNEY TO 1600 PENNSYLVANIA

Lying on our black leather couch in the living room, tears from my right eye are racing the tears that flow from my left eye down my cheeks. CNN has just announced that Senator Obama is the projected winner of Ohio in the 2008 Presidential election. This declaration assures him the historical victory.

I am wrestling with the emotions that have built up in my chest as they seek a way to escape; they seep out through my tears. I continue to struggle as I try to hold back the sobs that are welling up in me. In the middle of this internal altercation, my eight year old, Zion, walks into the room. Upon hearing that Senator Obama has won Ohio, he walks over to me, without saying a word. He bends down and he hugs me. His tight exaggerated hug conveys understanding that he couldn't possibly know. I hug him back thankful he is able to witness this at such a young age. I hold him close until the fountain in my eyes shuts off. We disconnect and my son retreats back to the den to watch Cartoon Network, without saying a word.

It is officially announced that Senator Obama is now President Elect Obama. He appears on stage in Chicago at Grant Park to give his acceptance speech with Michelle, Sasha, and Malia, and never have I seen such a powerful picture. The Obama's are the Huxtables times 1000. President Elect Obama gives his acceptance speech in the eloquent way we have come to expect and my cheeks are soaked again.

This time, Tai, my 12 year old comes over to me. He too, bends down and hugs me. As he hugs me, he simply says, "Let it out, Dad." He somehow knows I am trying to keep my composure, trying to push down the emotion that is once again erupting in my chest. It takes all the strength I have to avoid the Jesse Jackson ugly cry. But in the end it is useless. The tears gush as I hug my oldest son back.

While I am a wet mess on the couch, Shilease, is on the laptop looking for a hotel room for the inauguration. She secures the closest one we can find, in Baltimore Maryland and on January 20, 2009 we will be in D.C. to witness President Obama being sworn in at the Capital.

It is January 19, 2009 around 10:00pm and the four of us make it to our room in a Baltimore hotel. Shilease checks all the information and we decide to get up in four hours to start our journey into D.C.

At 2:00 a.m. we are up getting dressed and quickly walk out the door. We make it to the Green Belt train station by 3:30 a.m. (just when the parking lot is supposed to open). The parking lot is full.

We continue on to the next station at College Park; we get right into the garage and catch the first train to D.C. We exit the train station at The Federal Center and the station is packed with people. It is a claustrophobic's night terror. I feel pressure from the crowd that surrounds me from every side. We, and the crowd, gel in to one large mass as we make our way up the stairs and out to the street. I grab my youngest son's hand, Shilease grabs our oldest son's hand and she grabs my back pocket and we flow with the crowd. Once we break free of the station, it is instant relief and the crowd disperses into the city.

It is still night-time dark out, but the lights of the city are beautiful. We fall in line with the group and head towards the mall in front of the Capital Building. After some confusion, and an occasional area where people are close enough to you that you exchange DNA, we arrive on The Mall at about 5:30am. We camp out in the crowd in front of a large TV monitor, about a quarter mile away from the Capital Building. Once we stop moving, the cooler than normal January air attacks us.

All week the forecast was for temperatures in the 30's. Instead we get temperatures in the teens with a wind. Standing on The Mall in the large open field, the wind cuts you like a razor sharp, hot knife.

We are surrounded by people and the scene is unlike anything I have ever seen.

The most popular guy in the crowd is the guy giving out small American flags. People rush to him like he is handing out money. The second most popular guy is the businessman who thought ahead. He has boxes and boxes of hand warming packets for sale. I am sure, with just those around us, we pay for his child's college education.

To the right of us is a large group who is sitting on the ground wrapped in blankets. Behind us is a tall, heavy set white man who appears to be alone. He hands his nice, new, expensive video camera to a black teenaged girl. She is a stranger, before she holds the camera. He asks her to just film whatever she can until the battery runs out. He wants her to capture this day for him. In front of us, an Asian woman in her twenties has an autograph book that she is passing around to anyone who will sign it.

As we stand there, trying to forget the cold, someone begins singing, "We Shall Overcome" and the crowd joins in. The singing continues throughout the morning sporadically; mostly gospel songs. After about an hour, our youngest son decides to sit on the ground. He sits with his legs crossed, head down, hood up and hands in his coat. He falls asleep on the cold Mall gravel. Our oldest son decides to stand huddled close to Shilease and me.

People continue to pour into The Mall and walk through the crowd. We are packed so tightly that as they walk by they do not realize our eight year old is huddled on the ground. I station myself around him to prevent him from being stepped on. Shilease does the same and we cover him. A woman behind us takes up the job of traffic cop. She directs everyone who passes around our son who is camped out on the ground.

At about 8:00 am, after the sun has risen over the Capital Building, Shilease decides we have to move around and I agree.

By this point, I can feel my bone marrow freezing. I bend down to wake our little camper and at first he doesn't move. Immediately, I fear he has passed out because of the cold. After two or three shakes he rises and we begin to walk around. We walk toward the Capital Building and realize there still is plenty of room up ahead. Unfortunately, our eight year old is now shivering uncontrollably. Shilease and I decide we have to get him back to the hotel. We make our way off The Mall and soon we are in the middle of another mob. It appears several hundred people decide the cold wins at about the same time. This crowd is packed closer than any crowd we have faced yet. We don't move unless the mob says so and when the mob moves we obey. Suddenly, a large white man comes up behind Shilease and asks if she is trying to leave. Shilease replies, "I am just trying not to lose my children."

"Ok," he replies. "That guy in the red is about to open up a hole. Follow him."

The guy in the red instantly parts the crowd better than Moses parted the Red Sea. We shoot through the hole and are instantly off The Mall and the cool air feels good in my lungs.

Our plan is to walk back to the train station and catch the train back to Baltimore.

After walking all over D.C. for the next 90 minutes looking for a train station that has trains leaving the city, we find out that all the trains exiting the city are shut down until further notice. We are now trapped out in the cold.

Our youngest son, who is normally a talker hasn't said anything in the last 90 minutes. I look behind me and our oldest is now limping because his new boots are cutting in to his right heel. Shilease, who is usually the toughest of all of us, looks cold, miserable and worried about her boys. I am helpless and wonder why I even attempted this crazy outing.

As my protective husband and father's mind searches for a solution, I remember seeing a coach bus a few blocks back that had a small sign in the front window that read, "Warming bus." We make our way to 12th street and Pennsylvania and back to the bus. The driver opens the door and gladly welcomes us. The bus is running and warm. We take our seats, shed hats and gloves and let the warm air hit our cold skin.

The chairs are soft and comfortable and such a welcomed luxury. It is now about 10:00am and the driver puts in an old movie and we watch it on the many monitors on the bus. We all take a nap in the warmth.

At 11:00am the bus driver turns off the movie and turns on the radio. We hear play by play of where President Elect Obama is until he makes it to the Capital and the ceremony begins. I seat in my seat, with my head pressed against the cold glass of the window and I listen to what I thought was impossible.

My ears are flooded with the words of Pastor Rick Warren as he gives the opening prayer. My tears begin to flow, as I think about my 41 years of life. A life that began, with a cross burned on the lawn of my first home.

Aretha Franklin fills the bus with her beautiful voice, a voice I have heard so often growing up in Detroit, but today she sounds more pure than I ever remember. I reflected on my life to this point, to this day and I am overwhelmed. The constant battle between black and white in me and around me all vanishes. My heart leaps as Vice President Biden is sworn in and my heart beats with joy as President Obama says the sacred oath.

Several times, earlier in the day, I thought this trip was a huge mistake. Initially, I am heart broken because we aren't on The Mall when President Obama recites the oath. I realize where we are we are meant to be. We are on a quiet bus, warm and comfortable away from the distractions of a large crowd, away from the distractions like Aretha's hat that would steal attention away from this powerful moment in history. My good friend, Joe Tenbusch, later would point out the significance of being on a bus at this time and my heart understands this is no mistake.

Riding back to the hotel on the train, the scene on The Mall becomes much clearer. In the crowds so thick and so close the person next to me could hear my thoughts; I never heard one angry word. As the crowd pushed and it felt like I was going to implode from the pressure, no one ever got upset, no one yelled and my family and I were in a vacuum with two million other people. On this amazing day, not one person is arrested. I need to say that again because my mind can't comprehend that thought. Over two million people are gathered and not **_one_** person is arrested. I can almost assure you that at every sporting event I have ever gone to in my life, with more than five thousand people, someone was arrested.

The next day we return to D.C. to take the kids around to the different sites. Our first stop is the White House. Shilease and I have been there before, but this Wednesday in 2009 is special. We take pictures of the boys in front of the White House, and I imagine what President Obama and his family are doing in this beautiful home. I picture how nice it would be to be inside the White House, and I simply think to myself, "I will just wait until one of the boys gets elected."

This thought stops me—cold, and it has nothing to do with the temperature. I have never entertained that thought for myself. This impossible day never even penetrated my fantasies. It was too far out to even pretend for me. The ceiling that I grew up under is gone and my son's futures are limitless. LIMITLESS!

My black and white world is not the world my sons now live in. The struggle that Mom and Dad faced, behind the scenes, while I grew up will not be our boy's struggle. As a father, I am relieved that the ugly that walked side by side with us will not stalk my boys.

Racism is not erased. The heartbeat of prejudice is still beating but the change I've seen in 42 years is heart stopping.

We now live in a diverse neighborhood. The black neighborhood that the boys were born in became too much. Over the 13 years Shilease and I lived in this neighborhood, gradually, just as I saw Detroit ooze in to Shaftsbury Street as I was growing up, I saw hope exit the black neighborhood in Toledo.

As hope exited, despair replaced it and the "I will get you before you get me," mentality, that I remember from Whitcomb street, flowed down our street. Shilease and I make the decision to move to a more diverse neighborhood that leaves room for hope.

As the boys run out to play with their Black, White and Asian friends, I catch my tongue and hold it. The father in me wants to warn them of the dangers and prejudice that may be beyond our front door. I want to warn them of the pitfalls I experienced when I grew up. It takes all the strength in me to be silent. The realization that their time is different tells me to shut up.

"Their experience is not your experience. Don't taint them with your fears," wisdom tells me, as they head out the door for the park. Greater wisdom tells me someday, I will have to explain the truth and possibility of how race can affect them: to ignore that would be more tragic than tainting their safe world.

It doesn't matter if you agree with the selection of the 40th President or not. The fact that the majority of Americans said "Yes" to a black president has changed our world in ways I can't imagine. If you are American, that has to make you proud. It makes me proud to be a part of this time in history and thinking about what that means for my boys makes my cheeks moist again.

The extraordinary changes in America that have taken place throughout my life, causes me to reflect on the extraordinary results I have seen because of an extraordinary decision Mom and Dad made 42 years ago.

21

EXTRAORDINARY RESULTS

Grandma was right.

What Mom and Dad did was out of the ordinary. The one decision they made to put biracial on their list for potential adoptees which eventually led them to my adoption was extraordinary, not in a heroic sort of way but in an "out of the ordinary" way. Because this was such an out of the box, off the wall idea it changed the way they would look at things and that meant they would have to make some extraordinary decisions. Some of those decisions were agonizing I'm sure.

The decision to move to a black neighborhood to assure their new black child had a firm foundation was ground breaking. The thought that it had to be done even if it meant being at the expense of their white children I am sure was something they lost sleep over. The decision after five years of living in the black neighborhood to leave and move to a white neighborhood at the expense of their one black child but to preserve the family again stole many more nights of sleep. These decisions were extreme but necessary: extraordinary but vital and they were all rooted in the first decision that pushed this ball in motion. Many more similar life-changing decisions would come and go and after recounting this history, I sit and wonder was it all worth it. Was the cost of this one decision too expensive? Did the risks outweigh the gains?

A good friend of mine recently said to me, "You came out pretty normal growing up the way you did." On the surface he was right. I had come out closer to normal then you would expect.

But was that really true? This comment made me turn over in my mind if this was true. It caused me to dig deep to really challenge myself and to see if the surface matched my core. The desire to jump in waist deep into the life I had and really examine the results of a life as a transracial adoptee intrigued me. I began to examine just how I was affected by this unusual life and the results that flowed from it. In this examination, I hoped to find out if the price paid was too high.

I HAVE ISSUES

Driving down a dark highway four years ago, to a forgettable destination, I was listening to talk radio. The professional was talking about adoption. His theory was that a large majority of kids that have been adopted struggle with feelings of rejection and self-esteem issues. After about two minutes of listening to his theory, I concluded he had no idea what he was talking about and began surfing the radio for something that would keep my attention.

Over the next several weeks this theory kept coming back to me. After dismissing it as psycho-babble the first five or six times, I decided to entertain the thought that he may know a little of what he was talking about. The more I thought about it the more sense it made. In my own little quiet space I had to admit, I have issues.

My self-talk changed from, "There is no truth in this theory," into "There could be some sense in what he says." I began to surrender to the idea that a child may feel rejected after being given up for adoption.

The most powerful bond in nature is said to be between mother and child and if you are a child that was given up by his or her mother and placed for adoption, it is understandable that that child could have some feelings of rejection.

My next thought process was to think about it on a more personal level. I had to wrestle with the idea that *I* may have those issues. To this point, I liked the idea that I was basically unaffected by the adoption process and came through this crazy experience with no issues or scars.

This one statement by some unknown quack caused me to question if I was truly normal. I was in my thirties and I was finally at the age where I chose to look beyond the surface. How deep I would scratch below the surface was not known at this time, but I was open to doing a little probing

Part of me felt bad about giving into this thought. I was so blessed that I had landed with the family I had. I was so blessed to be adopted into a family that cared so strongly for me; a family that made so many unbelievable sacrifices for me. It felt like I was cheating on them for entertaining some of these feelings that I had buried for so long.

One conclusion I came up with was that the two were separate. The adoption experience was an amazing experience for me and a great success story. My family was great and loved me like no one else could. Period.

The deeper issues I may have are all right to feel. No matter how it happened or what the situation around it was, I had to deal with the fact that my mother gave me away. I did have some feelings of rejection. On the surface, I understood it was a very selfless act to give me up so I could have a better life than she thought she could give me. I understood it. I understood it. I understood it.

This understanding did not make the nagging go away. Over the next several months I came to accept I did have these feelings and that was all right. These feelings of rejection were identified and singular. They did not come with bitterness or anger. As I said, I understood the reasons behind the choice to give me up for adoption. My brain got it.

My heart mourned the loss of my biological mother and was stuck on being given away. The reasoning was simple, since my birth mother did not keep me and no one stole me from her, she gave me away.

When my heart spoke that truth to my brain, my brain understood the theory that from this comes feelings of rejection. How could you avoid those feelings?

How this feeling of rejection affected my life was my next puzzle. Did it really affect me? After turning it over and over in my mind I was able to come up with some very surprising examples.

What came to mind were several examples of how I stopped short of my potential in so many instances. I recalled the time in college when I was running track my freshman year. At a track meet during a race while on the track instead of turning as the track turned, I ran straight off the track and quit. On the surface it was simple. I was tired of running so I just stopped. There was more to it. Through the years I had become a master of justification. I told myself it was because this team was horrible. My high school track team could have beaten my college team easily. This was probably true but the deeper reason I quit was because I was afraid of succeeding.

The potential to be better than I had ever imagined was there. Deep down I knew if I committed to really working at it, I would be good, very good. That chance at being great scared me. So I did the easy thing; I pushed the buttons to activate the imploding sequence.

At the state meet in high school I did the same thing. I was less than twelve hours away from living up to my potential. My routine was simple and I did everything against it. Prior to this race everything I did was in preparation of the next race. The night before the race, I handed it away. Again the sequence was activated.

My professional working career followed the same pattern. I moved up quickly in my first job. All that I did was done to move up the corporate ladder. Just as I was about to really explode, the rebel in me purposely said the wrong thing to the wrong person and almost instantly my career that was skyrocketing was shut down.

The feeling of rejection manifested itself over and over again. My mind told me I was not good enough so whenever greatness was possible I quit. I found a way to step out before I found out if I could be great or not. Being my own enemy, there is no way to win.

This has continued as I have tried several businesses that never made it. Shilease and I started a stationary business that had potential to make us, at the minimum, some good side money. Before it took off, as I saw the potential I stopped working at it and let it dissolve.

Years later I discovered a hidden talent in working with wood. I began making these beautiful pieces of art made of wood. Everyone around me told me I should try and sell what I made, so I did. The work I did had potential to make a lot of money if marketed to the right people. The chance at success scared me off again. I put down the tools and justified it by saying no one will pay me what the pieces are worth; Again, another external excuse for my internal problem.

Then I developed the skill to make pens out of wood. Again this was a God given talent that just appeared out of thin air. There was a demand for the pens and their uniqueness made them valuable. Just as this new business was taking off, so did I. I put the tools down again and walked away.

While dating, this low self-esteem and feelings of rejection are why I felt the need to date several people at once. As I stated earlier, the attention I got from dating filled a void. The void's beginnings were rooted in these issues. I was afraid of rejection so I clung to more than one woman, that way; if one rejected me I still had the other. Dating more that one woman at a time also enacted the self-destruction sequence because it was always a matter of time before I was caught.

This book has been started and stopped many times, until finally I was sick and tired of being average. Underneath my issues I have always felt a calling to be great, a calling to be bigger than myself. That drive on the dark highway changed my life. The realization that I was my worst enemy in so many situations was frustrating and empowering. When you are the problem, you are also the solution.

If you are reading this book that you purchased in a bookstore or online, it is a testament that I conquered my fear of success. This is a great example of pushing past the voices that have always said, "You are not good enough. You do not deserve to be more than average." This project screams over the voices that I have given so much life to over the years.

Now that I know the root cause of my actions, I can change how I respond to things.

The inclination to drift in the direction that is less than me is still there. The fear of rejection causes me to shy away from relationships. The natural urge to go off by myself when in a crowded room or the urge to stay quiet instead of start up a conversation with someone still sits on my shoulder. This urge may never retreat, but now that I know it is there, I can push through it and force myself to act in a way that is more productive. The knowledge of my issues and their origin has been an empowering experience.

IN MY OWN SKIN

Towards the end of high school and through college, I went through my "black phase." There was a fear that my blackness would be rubbed off because I lived in an all white home environment. To combat that, I became black. My favorite T-shirt was a shirt I bought at the African Festival in Detroit. It was a black T-shirt that had the outline of Africa on the front. On the back it said, "It's a black thing you wouldn't understand." I would wear around my neck a leather medallion in the shape of Africa.

At about this time, I also was a part of a rap group called, General Principle. It was a group made up of friends from high school.

Derrick Louis was the leader and a group of us would sit and write lyrics to raps song. The raps were very pro-black and anti-white establishment. We often sat at the Hofmann dining room table and shared the raps we wrote. Mom would often be within ear shot and she would no doubt hear the venom we wrote.

My rap career was cut short when the other members of the group thought I sounded too proper. I was ruining the group's street credibility, so I was axed. Derrick, who had become a very close friend, sat me down and advised my services were no longer needed. Part of me was hurt because I still could not shake the anchor of talking proper. A larger part of me was relieved. The lyrics of our raps made me uneasy and I agreed I did lack the tough edge that the others in the group possessed.

There is no way, as I look back now, that I couldn't have offended Mom and Dad with my new "enlightened" path. They rode out this phase with me, allowing me to express myself in a not so productive way.

I created the fear that one color will drown out the other or water it down. My fear was that the result would be a shade in between the two, leaving me stuck in the middle not being comfortable or accepted in either shade.

The experience in college when I couldn't get along with the majority of the blacks at school concerned me. The majority of the blacks on campus did not want me around and the whites did not want me around either. The fear of being caught in the gap between the two was a real fear.

Later, I learned this was more a result of me not being friendly. The wall I put up worked well to keep people out, both white and black.

There are environments where I still feel uncomfortable. Being in an all white environment still makes me uneasy. The game of trying to figure out if a gesture or comment is racially motivated or the result of the person just not liking me, is still a game I struggle at.

There are some black environments that I find uncomfortable. There are situations where some blacks don't think I am black enough. When I was younger this would bother me because I hated being rejected because of something I had no control over. In recent years, it stopped bothering me. There is no way I will convince them otherwise and it isn't worth my time and energy.

The issues that I have and my maturation with myself are not issues that only I own. I realize many people who weren't adopted struggle with these same issues. My reflection on my life has pointed out to me that these are issues that have come from growing up as I did as an adoptee but I am not hoarding these issues as my own or as issues solely related to adoptees. I am also not blaming my adoption for my issues. I am simply stating these are things I have struggled with and this is where I think they are rooted. The fact that other people who weren't adopted struggle with these issues supports that I am not alone. This also supports the idea that I am more normal than not. If I didn't have issues, one could argue, that would make me more abnormal.

EXTRAORDINARY RESULTS

From the one extraordinary decision and the many extraordinary choices came some extraordinary results. If I was given the chance to start over in life, I would choose to change.... NOTHING. The love that I have received from my parents is overwhelming. I often ask myself, as a father, "Could I have made those sacrifices? "Could I have endured what Mom and Dad did for my boys?" Honestly, I just don't know.

The life that my sister Lisa, and brothers James and Matthew endured was not easy. They were forced to live life as a minority in several situations and for my brothers, especially; I know that was not always a setting they welcomed. I feel some responsibility for the struggles they were forced to endure because of me and have recently come to realize my brothers and I are not as close as I would like because of the life we lived. Their sacrifices may just have been too great.

Fortunately, my sister Lisa enjoyed the experiences. She recently told me she appreciated living life as a minority. She explained living as a minority really taught her what life is like for other people. Experiencing life as a minority for my sister was a positive and life changing experience, an experience she says she was fortunate to walk through. Regardless of how it was seen when we were going through it, the effects on our family and those around us are powerful.

To appreciate the extraordinary result, you need only look at the marriages and choices made by my family and the families around us.

My sister Lisa was the first to get married. She married a black man she met while in the Air Force. They have a beautiful biracial daughter.

James married a woman from China and they have a daughter as well.

Matthew married a woman from China also. They have a son. Their marriage didn't last and Matthew remarried. In his second marriage, Matthew married a woman from Japan. They have a son and a daughter.

The colors of our family are obvious and a testament to the beautiful lessons we learned growing up. Whether they agreed with our upbringing or not, you can't help but see the affects our life had on their adult life.

The marriage of color has extended to my close friends from Shaftsbury.

My best friend Mike married a woman from Puerto Rico and they have two girls and one boy. Mike co-founded a non-profit agency in inner city Detroit that helps thousands of children every year.

Mike's younger brother, Joe majored in African Studies at the University of Michigan and still knows more about my culture than I do. He married a woman from Hungary and they later divorced. He is now a principal at a black high school in Chicago. He too lives a life rich with color.

Jose Galano, the boy I flipped off the first week I moved to Shaftsbury Street grew up and married a woman from the Detroit area, who is white, and they adopted two children from Guatemala. The evolution of Jose makes me tear up when I think of the change that I had the privilege of witnessing. Jose is the friend and brother I am most proud of.

The tree that was planted when my Mom and Dad adopted me grew and grew and spawned branch after branch that went in so many directions. I laugh today when I look at my immediate family. Besides Mom and Dad, I was the only one who married in the same race.

Three years ago, Grandma died. The last days of her life she was a very difficult person to be around. She was always very judgmental of everyone throughout her life. Now her increasing age gave her the excuse to say anything to anybody. She made life at the nursing home hell for my mother, who cared for her daily, and the nursing home staff.

In the last three years of her life whenever I saw her she would make sure to comment on how much weight I had gained. (Another form of my sabotage) I had grown accustomed to her criticism and chose to deal with it by seeing her less and less.

Grandma's critiques continued every time I saw her in the nursing home. They were not racially motivated. I knew that, but I was just tired of hearing about how fat I was.

The last time I saw grandma alive she was lying in her bed at the nursing home. She was in and out of sleep. When she woke up, I was standing at the end of her bed and she looked at me. She reached for me and I moved towards her and grabbed her hand. Her hands were like Aunt Theresa's and Aunt Ruth's from years ago. They were worn and soft and covered with loose skin.

Grandma looked me in my face and quietly said, "Oh Kevin, you look ok."

Where she used to say, "Oh Kevin, you're still putting on the weight," or something similar, she said I looked "Ok."

On the ride home, my wife Shilease explained to me the significance of what Grandma said. I was so conditioned to being called fat I was just relieved she did not do it again.

Grandma was saying so much more in the only way she knew how. These were the last words Grandma said to me and I am still trying to come to the same realization.

The changes I saw in friends and family, the street and community that I saw change, and the changes I have felt within my own chest make it easy to answer the questions that began this chapter. Because of this one extraordinary decision made over 40 years ago I have been fortunate to witness many extraordinary results from an extraordinary life growing up black in white.